MySpace™

VISUAL™

Quick Tips

Visual

by Paul McFedries and
Sherry Willard Kinkoph

D0123856

WILEY

Wiley Publishing, Inc.

MySpace™ VISUAL™ Quick Tips

Published by
Wiley Publishing, Inc.
111 River Street
Hoboken, NJ 07030-5774

Published simultaneously in Canada

Copyright © 2006 by Wiley Publishing, Inc.,
Indianapolis, Indiana

Library of Congress Control Number: 2006929470

ISBN-13: 978-0-470-08969-9

ISBN-10: 0-470-08969-5

Manufactured in the United States of America

10 9 8 7 6 5 4 3 2 1

1K/QR/QY/QW/IN

Trademark Acknowledgments

Contact Us

For general information on our other products and
services contact our Customer Care Department within
the U.S. at 800-762-2974, outside the U.S. at 317-572-
3993, or fax 317-572-4002.

For technical support please visit www.wiley.com/
techsupport.

TK
5105.88
. M36
2006

1376665

WILEY

Wiley Publishing, Inc.

Sales

Contact Wiley
at (800) 762-2974 or
fax (317) 572-4002.

Praise for Visual Books

"I have to praise you and your company on the fine products you turn out. I have twelve Visual books in my house. They were instrumental in helping me pass a difficult computer course. Thank you for creating books that are easy to follow. Keep turning out those quality books."

Gordon Justin (Brielle, NJ)

"What fantastic teaching books you have produced! Congratulations to you and your staff. You deserve the Nobel prize in Education. Thanks for helping me understand computers."

Bruno Tonon (Melbourne, Australia)

"A Picture Is Worth A Thousand Words! If your learning method is by observing or hands-on training, this is the book for you!"

Lorri Pegan-Durastante (Wickliffe, OH)

"Over time, I have bought a number of your 'Read Less - Learn More' books. For me, they are THE way to learn anything easily. I learn easiest using your method of teaching."

José A. Mazón (Cuba, NY)

"You've got a fan for life!! Thanks so much!!"

Kevin P. Quinn (Oakland, CA)

"I have several books from the Visual series and have always found them to be valuable resources."

Stephen P. Miller (Ballston Spa, NY)

"I have several of your Visual books and they are the best I have ever used."

Stanley Clark (Crawfordville, FL)

"Like a lot of other people, I understand things best when I see them visually. Your books really make learning easy and life more fun."

John T. Frey (Cadillac, MI)

"I have quite a few of your Visual books and have been very pleased with all of them. I love the way the lessons are presented!"

Mary Jane Newman (Yorba Linda, CA)

"Thank you, thank you, thank you...for making it so easy for me to break into this high-tech world."

Gay O'Donnell (Calgary, Alberta, Canada)

"I write to extend my thanks and appreciation for your books. They are clear, easy to follow, and straight to the point. Keep up the good work! I bought several of your books and they are just right! No regrets! I will always buy your books because they are the best."

Seward Kollie (Dakar, Senegal)

"I would like to take this time to thank you and your company for producing great and easy-to-learn products. I bought two of your books from a local bookstore, and it was the best investment I've ever made! Thank you for thinking of us ordinary people."

Jeff Eastman (West Des Moines, IA)

"Compliments to the chef!! Your books are extraordinary! Or, simply put, extra-ordinary, meaning way above the rest! THANKYOU THANKYOU THANKYOU! I buy them for friends, family, and colleagues."

Christine J. Manfrin (Castle Rock, CO)

Credits

Project Editor
Sarah Hellert

Acquisitions Editor
Jody Lefevere

Product Development Supervisor
Courtney Allen

Copy Editor
Scott Tullis

Editorial Manager
Robyn Siesky

Business Manager
Amy Knies

Editorial Assistant
Laura Sinise

Special Help
Barb Moore

Manufacturing
Allan Conley
Linda Cook
Paul Gilchrist
Jennifer Guynn

Book Design
Kathie Rickard

Production Coordinator
Kristie Rees

Layout
Amanda Spagnuolo

Screen Artist
Jill A. Proll

Illustrator
Cheryl Grubbs

Cover Design
Mike Trent

Proofreader
Laura L. Bowman

Quality Control
Laura Albert
Leeann Harney

Indexer
Infodex Indexing Services Inc.

Vice President and Executive Group Publisher
Richard Swadley

Vice President and Publisher
Barry Pruett

Composition Director
Debbie Stailey

About the Authors

Paul McFedries is the president of Logophilia Limited, a technical writing company. Paul has written nearly 50 books that have sold over 3 million copies worldwide. His current titles include the Wiley books *Teach Yourself VISUALLY Windows XP, 2nd Edition, Teach Yourself VISUALLY Computers, 4th Edition, Windows XP: Top 100 Simplified Tips & Tricks, 2nd Edition,* and *Excel PivotTables and PivotCharts: Your visual blueprint for creating dynamic spreadsheets.* Paul is also the proprietor of Word Spy, a Web site devoted to new words and phrases (see www.wordspy.com). Paul lives in Toronto with his wonderful wife, Karen, and their silly dog, Gypsy.

Sherry Willard Kinkoph has written and edited oodles of books over the past 10 years covering a variety of computer topics, including Microsoft Office programs. Her recent titles include *Teach Yourself VISUALLY Photoshop Elements 3.0* and *Office 2003 Simplified.* Sherry's ongoing quest is to help users of all levels master ever-changing computer technologies. No matter how many times they — the software manufacturers and hardware conglomerates — throw out a new version or upgrade, Sherry vows to be there to make sense of it all and help computer users get the most out of their machines.

How To Use This Book

MySpace VISUAL Quick Tips includes tasks that reveal cool secrets, teach timesaving tricks, and explain great tips guaranteed to make you more productive with MySpace. The easy-to-use layout lets you work through all the tasks from beginning to end or jump in at random.

Who Is This Book For?

If you want to know the basics about MySpace, or if you want to learn shortcuts, tricks, and tips that let you work smarter and faster, this book is for you. And because you learn more easily when someone *shows* you how, this is the book for you.

Conventions Used In This Book

❶ Introduction
The introduction is designed to get you up to speed on the topic at hand.

❷ Steps
This book uses step-by-step instructions to guide you easily through each task. Numbered callouts on every screen shot show you exactly how to perform each task, step by step.

❸ Tips
Practical tips provide insights to save you time and trouble, caution you about hazards to avoid, and reveal how to do things with MySpace that you never thought possible!

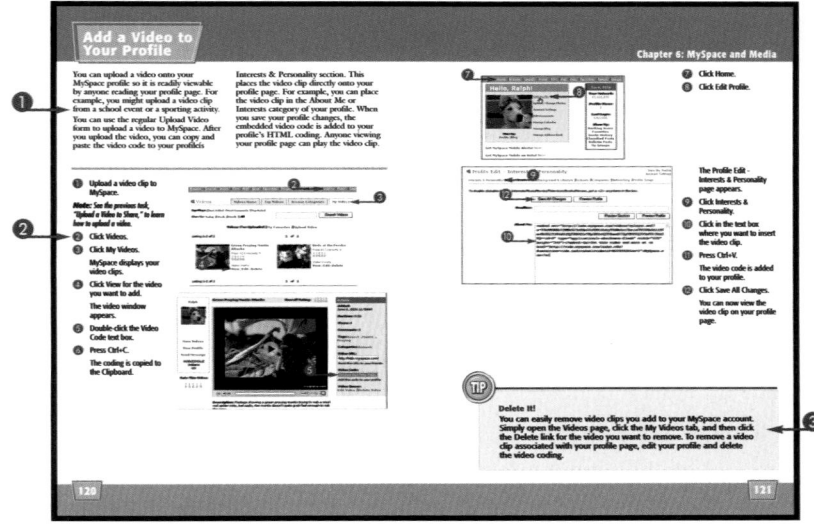

Table of Contents

chapter 5 **Blogging with MySpace**

chapter 6 **MySpace and Media**

chapter 7 Working with MySpace Events

chapter 8 Maintaining Privacy on MySpace

chapter 9 Enhancing MySpace Security

Chapter 1

Setting Up Your Profile

When you set up your MySpace account, you get a basic profile with your name, your picture, and a few contact links. To make your MySpace profile *your* space, you need to customize. Chapters 2 and 3 offer some powerful profile customization tips, but this chapter gets you off to a more leisurely start with a few simple customizations. For example, you will learn how to change your profile name, how to get a custom MySpace Web address, and how to add more photos to your site and use one of those photos as your new profile picture. You will also learn how to specify a networking category, set up an offline message, and cancel your account if things do not work out.

Quick Tips

Change Your Profile Display Name

You can change your profile display name to something that better suits you or the topic of your MySpace Web site.

When you sign up for a MySpace account, one of the first things you specify is a name that you want the MySpace world to know you as. This name appears at the top of your profile, above your picture.

Because your MySpace profile acts as a kind of online persona, it is possible that the persona you want the world to see may change after a while. If that happens, then you might want to change your display name to something more suited to the new you or to the new theme of your profile.

---

① In MySpace, click Home.

② Click Edit Profile.

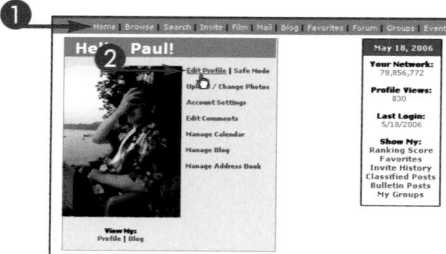

The Profile Edit - Interests & Personality page appears.

③ Click Name.

④ Type the new display name.

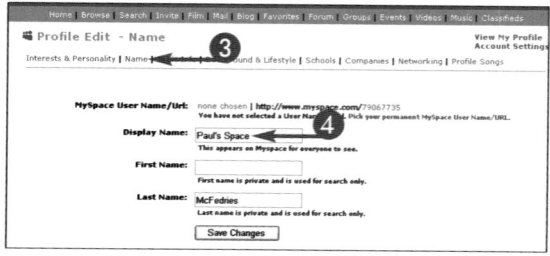

⑤ Click Save Changes.

MySpace updates your profile.

⑥ Click View My Profile.

● Your profile appears with the new display name.

Note: *In Chapter 3, see the "Replace Your Profile Name with a Custom Image" task to learn how to use an image in place of your name.*

TIP

More Options!
By default, you do not have any way to customize the look of your profile name, just the text itself. Note, however, that MySpace only allows a maximum of 50 characters for the name. If you would like to dress up your name with fonts and colors, see the first three tasks in Chapter 2.

Get a Custom Web Address for Your Profile

You can make it easier to direct other people to your MySpace profile by setting up a custom MySpace Web address.

When you first sign up with MySpace, they assign you an eight-digit "friend ID," and that ID is used as the address of your profile. Here is an example:

www.myspace.com/77453322

Having a number as part of your address makes your address nearly impossible for

other people to remember. To solve this problem, you can sign up for a custom MySpace Web address, which looks something like this:

www.myspace.com/*MyProfile*

In an actual address, the *MyProfile* part would be some name that you specify. This is much easier to remember, so having such an address makes it simple to send people to your profile.

---

① In MySpace, click Home.

② Click Edit Profile.

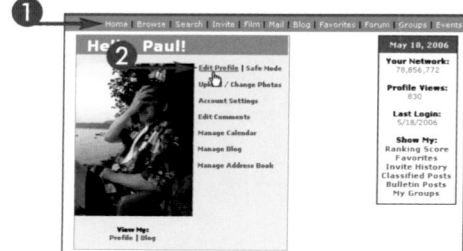

The Profile Edit - Interests & Personality page appears.

③ Click Name.

④ Click Pick Your Permanent MySpace User Name/URL.

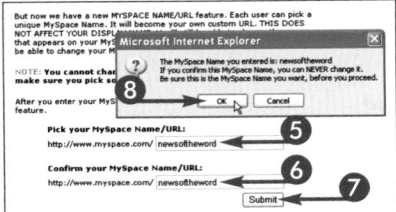

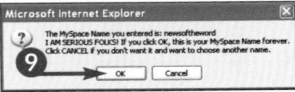

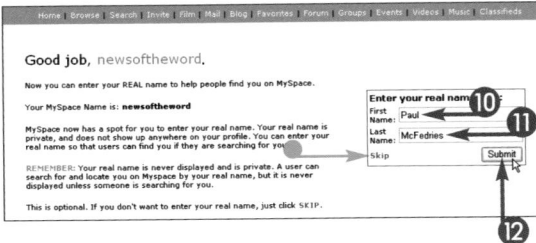

⑤ Type the text you want to use for your address.

⑥ Type the text again.

⑦ Click Submit.

MySpace warns you that you can never change the address.

⑧ Click OK.

MySpace warns you again that you can never change the address.

⑨ Click OK.

● If you do not want to give MySpace your real name, click Skip.

⑩ Type your first name.

⑪ Type your last name.

⑫ Click Submit.

MySpace shows your new MySpace address.

Caution!
As the warnings that the MySpace displays indicate, you cannot change your Web address once you select it. If you decide you prefer a different address, you have no choice but to start up a new MySpace account. Therefore, give serious thought to the address you prefer before committing to it.

Upload Photos to Your Profile

You can give your profile visitors some good eye candy by uploading a lot of pictures to your profile.

In your main profile page, visitors can then click the Pics link on your profile page to view images you have uploaded to your profile. By default, the Pics page contains only the image you uploaded when you first signed up with MySpace.

However, MySpace allows you to upload other photos to your profile. Having a lot of interesting and fun images can really make your site popular.

Note that you cannot upload images of cartoons, celebrities, nudity, or pornography, or copyrighted images. The images must be less than 600KB and must be in either the JPEG or GIF format.

---

① In MySpace, click Home.

② Click Upload / Change Photos.

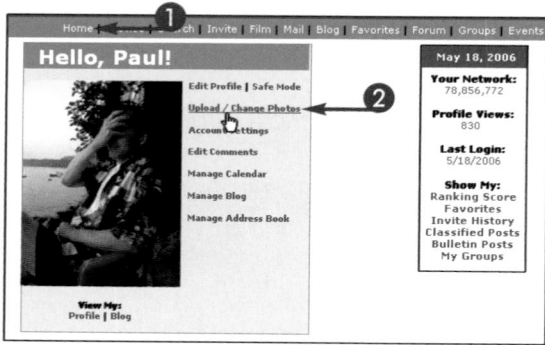

The Upload Your Photo page appears.

③ Click Browse.

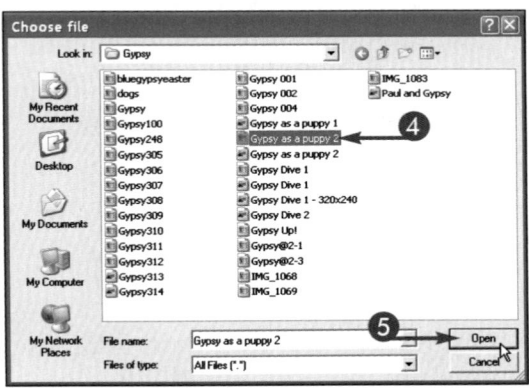

The Choose File dialog box appears.

④ Click the file you want to upload.

⑤ Click Open.

● The file path appears in the text box.

⑥ Click Upload.

MySpace uploads the file to your profile.

More Options!

You can make your photos more interesting by adding captions that describe, date, or title the images. Follow Steps **1** and **2** to display the Upload Your Photo page. Scroll down the page until you see the photo with which you want to work, and then click Add Caption. Type the caption in the text box that appears, and then click Update Caption. When MySpace asks you to confirm, click Post Caption.

Change Your Default Profile Picture

You can present a different face to the MySpace world by changing your default profile image.

When you signed up for your MySpace account, you were given the opportunity to upload a picture to MySpace, and that picture became the image that appears on your main profile page. This picture also appears when you send messages, friend requests, bulletins, and invitations,

post to a group, and when people use the MySpace Browse feature to look for your profile. In other words, your default profile photo is your MySpace "face."

If you have uploaded other photos — as described in the previous task — then you may have a new image that you think is more suitable to appear as your MySpace image. If so, then you can change your default photo to the new image.

① Click Home.

② Click Upload / Change Photos.

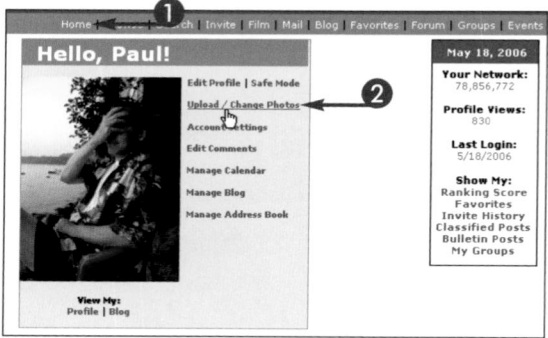

The Upload Your Photo page appears.

③ Below the image you want to use for your profile, click Set As Default.

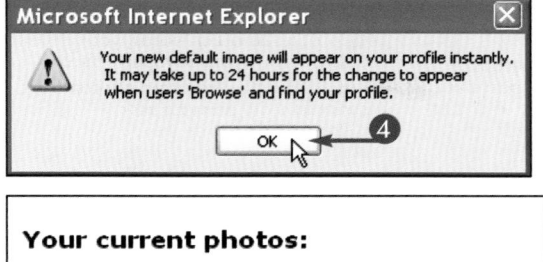

MySpace warns you that it may take up to 25 hours for other users to see the new picture when they use Browse to find you.

④ Click OK.

● MySpace adds "This is currently your profile image" under the photo.

More Options!

If you have photos that you no longer want others to view, you should delete them to reduce the amount of time it takes for your Pics page to load. Follow Steps **1** and **2** to display your uploaded photos, and then click Delete under a photo you no longer need. Click OK when MySpace asks you to confirm.

Specify a Networking Affiliation for Your Profile

You can contact people in the same line of work as you by specifying the field in which you work and what you do in that field.

Although MySpace is a great way to meet new friends, it is also a good source for new career opportunities. If you specify your line of work — what MySpace calls your networking affiliation — you can then search for other MySpace members in the same line of work and make contact with any that look interesting or promising.

The first step is to specify your networking affiliation, which means the field in which you work, the sub-field, and the role you play. You can then search on this information, which is covered in the next task.

---

① Click Home.

② Click Edit Profile.

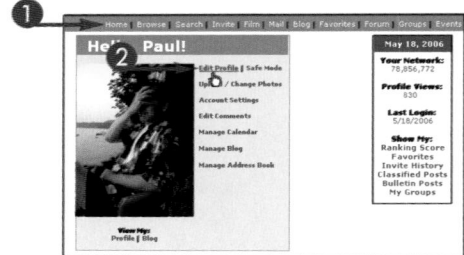

The Profile Edit - Interests & Personality page appears.

③ Click Networking.

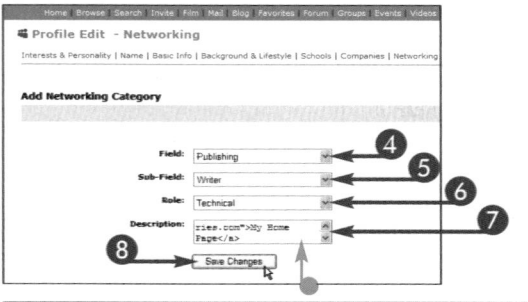

④ In the Field list, click the field in which you work.

⑤ In the Sub-Field list, click the sub-field in which you work.

⑥ In the Role list, click your role at work.

⑦ Type a description for your work.

● To include a link to your home page, type the following in the Description box (replace *URL* with the address):

```
<a href="URL">
My Home Page</a>
```

⑧ Click Save Changes.

● MySpace adds the networking affiliation to your profile.

More Options!
If you want to use MySpace for networking, be sure to let everyone who views your profile know that. Click Home, click Edit Profile, and then click Basic Info. In the Basic Information window, scroll down to the I Am Here For section and click Networking (☐ changes to ☑).

Find People for Networking

You can enhance your career prospects by using the MySpace Search feature to look for members who are in the same line of work as you.

You saw in the previous task that you can update your profile to include your networking affiliation: your work field, sub-field, and role. After you have done that, you may receive messages or friend requests from people in the same line of work. However, why wait to be contacted? You can use the MySpace Search feature to display a list of members who are in the same line of work. Of course, your networking searches are not limited to people who do the same job as you. For example, if you are a writer, you may be interested in contacting acquisitions editors or publishers.

---

1 Click Search.

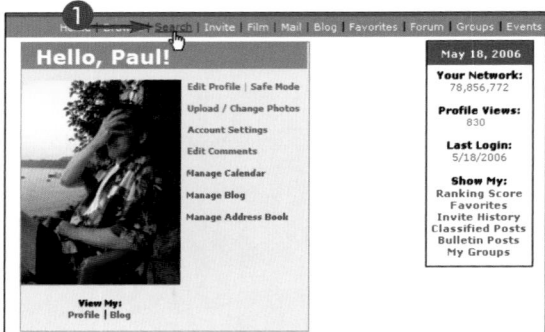

The MySpace Search page appears.

2 In the Field list, click the field you want to search.

3 In the Sub-Field list, click the sub-field you want to search.

4 In the Role list, click the role you want to search.

5 Type an optional keyword to narrow your search.

6 Click Find.

MySpace displays the search results.

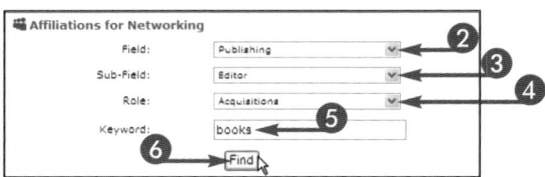

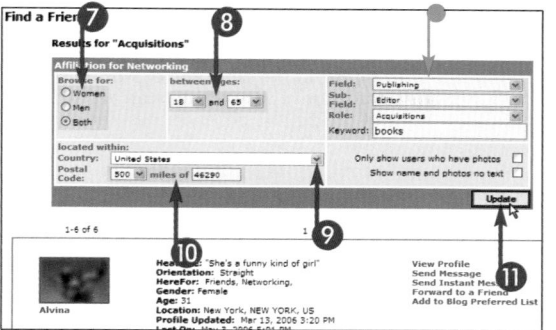

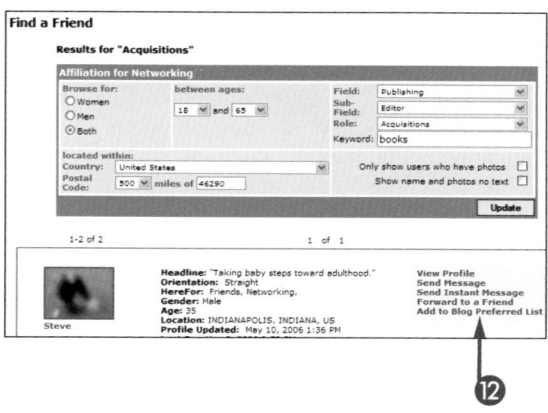

- MySpace displays enhanced Affiliation for Networking search options so you can refine your search.

⑦ Under Browse For, specify Women, Men, or Both (○ changes to ◉).

⑧ Under Between Ages, click to specify an age range.

⑨ In the Country list, click to specify a country.

⑩ In the Postal Code list, click to specify a distance from a ZIP code.

⑪ Click Update.

MySpace displays the revised search results.

⑫ Use these links to contact a person with whom you want to network.

Try This!

If you want to find members with the same field, sub-field, or role as you, MySpace offers a quick method. In your profile, scroll down to the Networking section, and then click your field, sub-field, or role. MySpace runs a search for members who have the same networking affiliation as the one you clicked.

Set Up a Message to Display When You Are Offline

You can set up a message that people see when they view your profile while you are not online.

When people view your profile, MySpace displays an Online icon next to your picture when you are signed in, and nothing if you are not. For something a little friendlier, you can configure your account to display a message when you are offline. This is usually called an *away message*. Your away message appears at the top of your profile.

You can also configure your account to not accept any new messages while you are offline. If other users click your Send a Message link, they just see your away message, instead.

① Click Home.

② Click Account Settings.

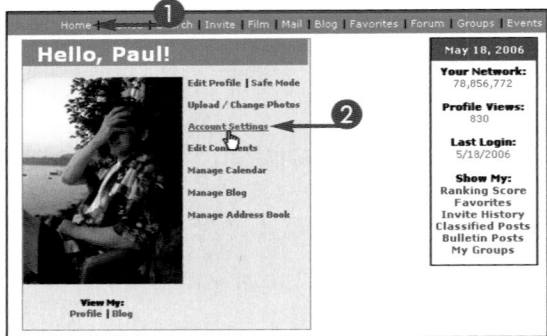

The Change Account Settings page appears.

③ Click View / Edit Away Message.

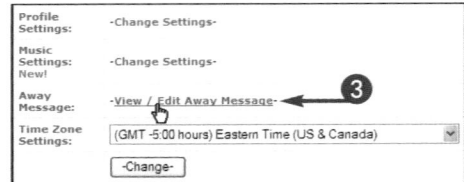

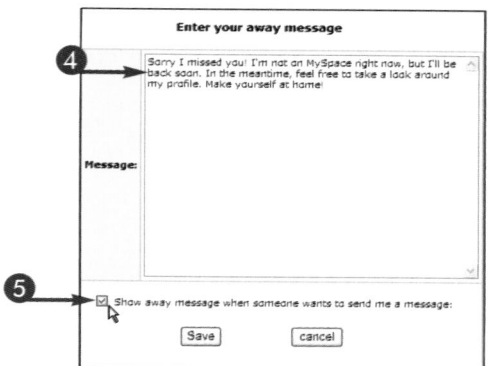

The Enter Your Away Message page appears.

④ Click inside the Message box and type your message.

⑤ Click here if you want other people to see your message when they try to contact you (☐ changes to ☑).

⑥ Click Save.

MySpace saves your away message.

Check This Out!

Crafting an interesting or funny away message is an art in itself, and there are many sites on the Web devoted to recording the best away messages. Many are aimed at instant messaging programs, but you can adapt the messages to MySpace easily enough. See www.awaymessages.com or www.awaybox.com. You can also run a Google search on the phrase "away messages."

Cancel Your MySpace Account

You can cancel your MySpace account if you want to start over with a fresh profile. The first part of this chapter explained how to get a custom MySpace address for your profile. If you went through the steps in that task, you saw that MySpace warns you *twice* that you cannot change your address after you select it. So what

do you do if you do not like the address you picked or if the address no longer fits the theme of your profile? Your only choice is to start over with a new account and then choose a different address. After you get your new profile set up, you can then delete your old MySpace account.

---

① Click Home.

② Click Account Settings.

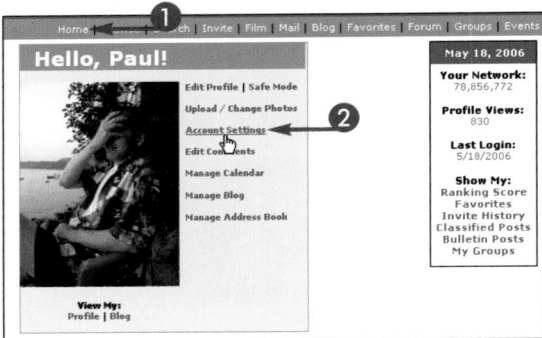

The Change Account Settings page appears.

③ Click Cancel Account.

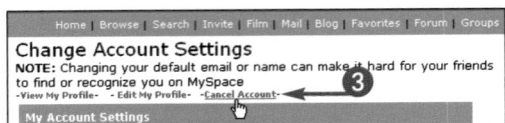

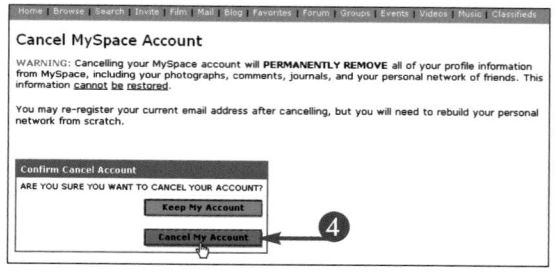

The Cancel MySpace Account page appears.

④ Click Cancel My Account.

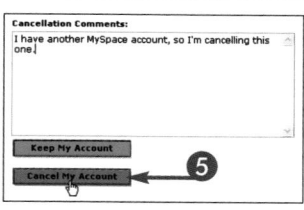

MySpace asks you to explain why you are cancelling and to confirm that you want to cancel.

⑤ Click Cancel My Account.

Caution!

If you have important information on your MySpace profile that you want to preserve, be sure to copy that information to your computer before you cancel your account. Once you cancel your MySpace account, all your blog posts and other data get deleted, so be sure to save what you need.

continued

You can also cancel your MySpace account if you want to leave the service.

Some people find that MySpace is a great deal of fun at first, but then it becomes less exciting over time. Most people do not have the time to keep up with a blog, which requires regular posts to keep an audience. Other people get tired of the constant spam messages, group invitations, rude comments, and other negative aspects of MySpace. You can prevent many of these unwanted messages by making your MySpace account more private (see Chapter 8) and more secure (see Chapter 9).

MySpace sends you an e-mail message to confirm the cancellation.

⑥ Switch to your e-mail program.

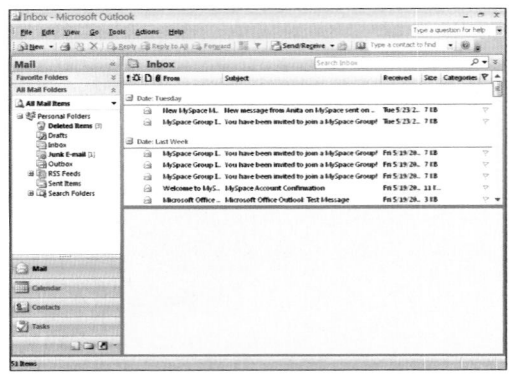

⑦ When the cancellation message arrives, click the message.

⑧ Click the cancellation link in the message.

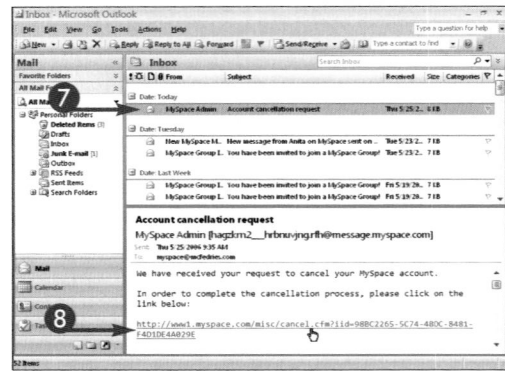

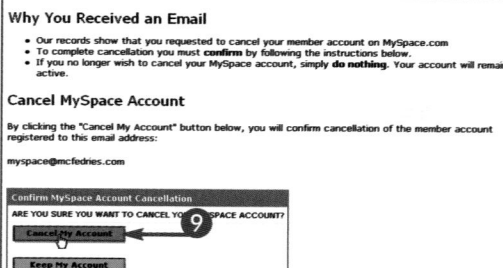

MySpace asks you again to confirm that you want to cancel.

9 Click Cancel My Account.

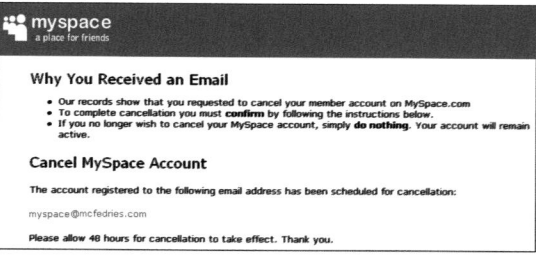

MySpace cancels your account.

Important!

When you cancel your account, MySpace warns you that you must wait 48 hours if you want to create a new MySpace account using the same e-mail address as you used for your cancelled account. However, that is hardly ever the case. Most of the time, you can reuse your old MySpace e-mail address right away.

Customizing Your Profile Text

You can make your profile easier to read and better looking by customizing the look of the text.

Customizing text mostly involves changing the font, size, and color of the text. As you learn in this chapter, you can apply these changes to any text in your profile, including your profile name, the module titles, headings, and text, the Extended Network and blurb text, and all the links that appear throughout your profile.

In this chapter, you also learn how to use HTML tags to customize your text, how to create a "Top 10" list of items, how to put together a bulleted list, and how to include a scrolling text marquee. (If you want to learn more about HTML and style sheets, please see *Teach Yourself VISUALLY HTML*, by Sherry Kinkoph.)

Quick Tips

Customize Your Profile Text Font

You can add text appeal to your profile by customizing the font used to display your text.

The default font used in MySpace profiles is not very attractive, so you should consider changing the font to something that is easier on the eyes. To do this, you use the `font-family` style and set it to the typeface you want. Most MySpace designers specify several typefaces because a user may not have your favorite typeface installed:

```
{font-family: Verdana, Helvetica, Arial;}
```

To use this style for most of your profile text, apply it to the `td` element. For the text beside your profile image, apply the style to the `.text` class.

---

① In MySpace, click Home.

② Click Edit Profile.

The Profile Edit - Interests & Personality page appears.

③ In the About Me text box, type the opening and closing `style` tags.

④ Type the `font-family` style for the `td` element and `.text` class.

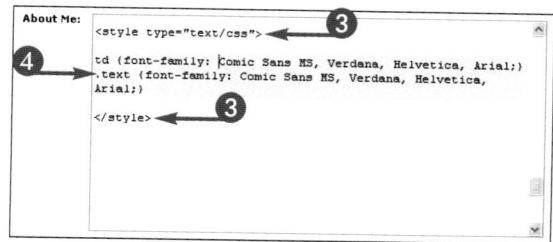

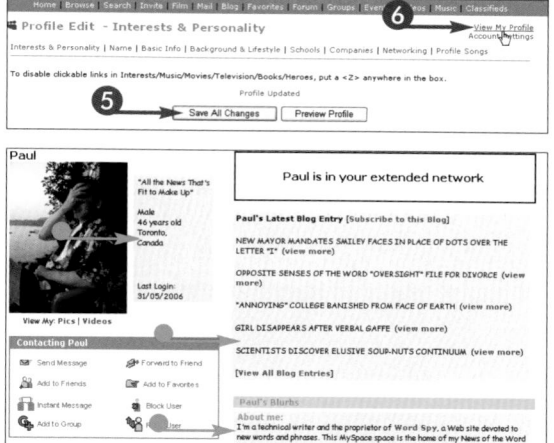

5 Click Save All Changes.

MySpace updates your profile.

6 Click View My Profile.

● Your profile appears with the new font applied.

More Options!

Applying the `font-family` style to the `td` element and `.text` class does not affect the text in the MySpace URL box. To change the font in that box, apply the `font-family` style to the `div` element, as in this example:

```
div {font-family: Verdana, Helvetica, Arial;}
```

25

You can make your profile text easier to read by increasing the text size.

The default text size for most of the profile text is only 8 points, which is a bit too small, particularly for readers using a high screen resolution. Increasing the text size will help those visitors read your text. You can also adjust the text size to make certain parts of your profile stand out.

To adjust the text size, set the `font-size` style to a value expressed in points. For example, to set the text size to 10 points, you would use the following code:

```
{font-size: 10pt;}
```

As in the previous task, here you will apply the `font-size` style to the `td` element and the `.text` class.

---

① In MySpace, click Home.

② Click Edit Profile.

The Profile Edit - Interests & Personality page appears.

③ In the About Me text box, type the opening and closing `style` tags.

④ Type the `font-size` style for the `td` element and `.text` class.

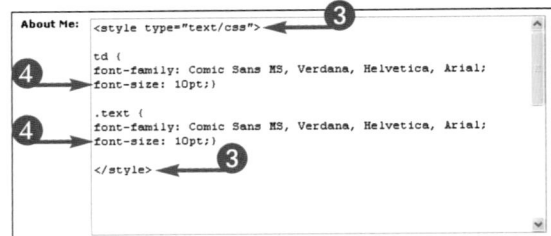

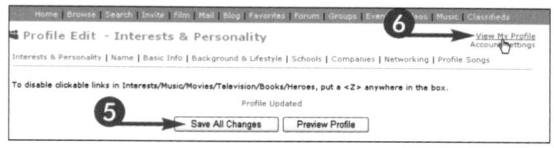

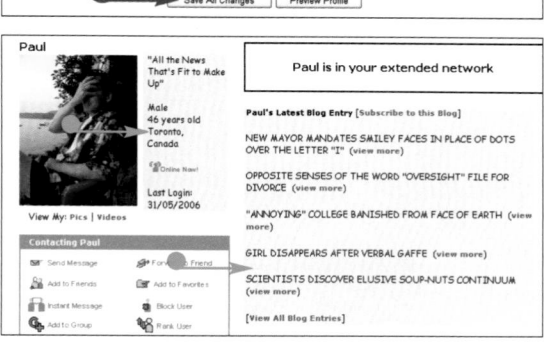

⑤ Click Save All Changes.

MySpace updates your profile.

⑥ Click View My Profile.

● Your profile appears with the new text size applied.

More Options!

Applying the `font-size` style to the `td` element and `.text` class does not affect your profile name. To change the text size of your name, apply the `font-size` style to the `.nametext` class, as in this example:

`.nametext {font-size: 18pt;}`

You can give your profile a more consistent look by changing the text colors to match.

The default text color scheme in a MySpace profile is a mish-mash of blue, black, white, orange, and red, and it is probably the thing that MySpace users hate the most. Fortunately, you can create a more consistent and coherent color scheme by changing the colors of the various profile elements.

To adjust the text color, set the `color` style to either a color name or to a value in the RRGGBB format, where RR is a two-digit hexadecimal value for red, GG is a two-digit hexadecimal value for green, and BB is a two-digit hexadecimal value for blue:

```
td {color: DarkBlue;}
.text {color: 228822;}
```

① In MySpace, click Home.

② Click Edit Profile.

The Profile Edit - Interests & Personality page appears.

③ In the About Me text box, type the opening and closing `style` tags.

④ Type the `color` style for the `td` element and `.text` class.

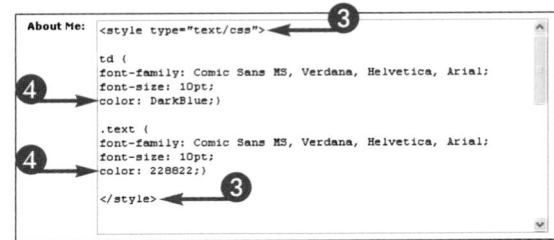

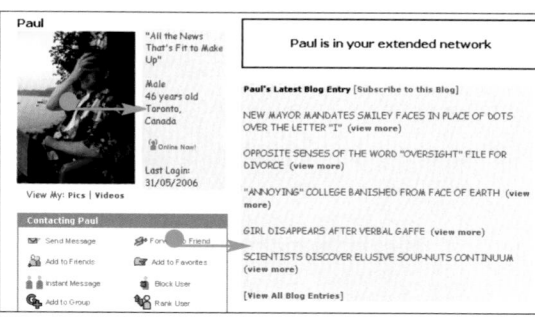

5 Click Save All Changes.

MySpace updates your profile.

6 Click View My Profile.

● Your profile appears with the new text color applied.

Check This Out!

There are thousands of colors you can apply to your profile text. However, only about 140 of those colors have names that you can use with the color style. To see a list of those names (and the corresponding RRGGBB values for each color), see the following Web page:

www.mcfedries.com/CreatingAWebPage/x11colors.asp

You can spruce up your profile's module titles and headings by changing the text font, size, and color.

The left side of your profile displays a series of modules: Interests, Details, Schools, Networking, and Companies. Each module has a title, and some modules have headings — for example, the Interests module has the headings General, Music, Movies, and so on.

To change the text for the titles, you apply the `font-family`, `font-size`, and `color` styles to the `.whitetext12` class. To change the text for the headings, you apply the same styles to the `.lightbluetext8` class. Note, too, that if you want the titles centered, you can also add the following style to the `.whitetext12` class:

```
text-align: center;
display: block;
```

1 In MySpace, click Home.

2 Click Edit Profile.

The Profile Edit - Interests & Personality page appears.

3 In the About Me text box, type the opening and closing `style` tags.

4 Type the styles for the `.whitetext12` class.

5 Type the styles for the `.lightbluetext8` class.

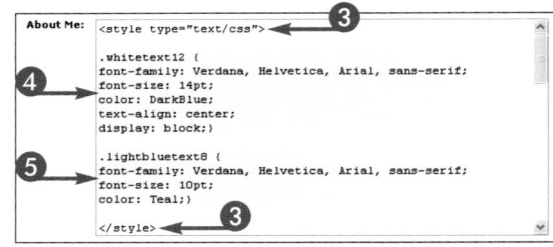

```
About Me:  <style type="text/css">

.whitetext12 {
font-family: Verdana, Helvetica, Arial, sans-serif;
font-size: 14pt;
color: DarkBlue;
text-align: center;
display: block;}

.lightbluetext8 {
font-family: Verdana, Helvetica, Arial, sans-serif;
font-size: 10pt;
color: Teal;}

</style>
```

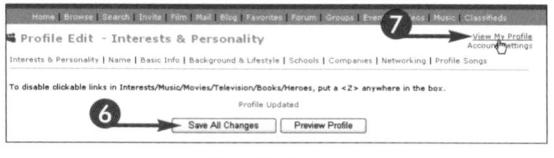

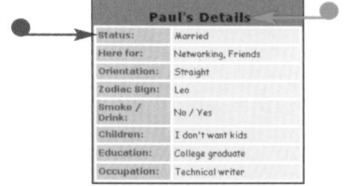

6️⃣ Click Save All Changes.

MySpace updates your profile.

7️⃣ Click View My Profile.

● Your profile appears with the text styles applied to the `.whitetext12` class.

● Your profile appears with the text styles applied to the `.lighbluetext8` class.

More Options!
You can also control text bolding by using the `font-weight` style, which you set to one of the following values: `lighter`, `normal`, `bold`, or `bolder`:

`{font-weight: bold;}`

For italics, apply `font-style` as follows:

`{font-style: italic;}`

You can give your profile a more consistent look by changing the font of your Interests to match your other profile text.

If you have been modifying the font, size, and color of your profile text as described in the past few tasks, you may be wondering why the text in your Interests module is not affected. That is because

MySpace sets up each item you list as an Interest as a link — when you click one of those links, MySpace shows you a list of members who share the same interest.

To modify your Interests link text, you need to apply the `font-family`, `font-size`, and `color` styles to the `a.searchlinkSmall` class.

---

① In MySpace, click Home.

② Click Edit Profile.

The Profile Edit - Interests & Personality page appears.

③ In the About Me text box, type the opening and closing `style` tags.

④ Type the styles for the `a.searchlinkSmall` class.

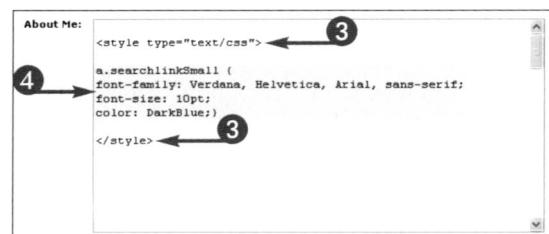

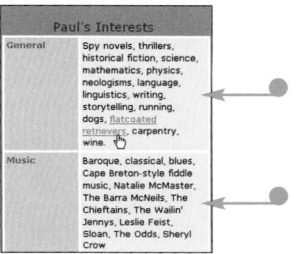

⑤ Click Save All Changes.

MySpace updates your profile.

⑥ Click View My Profile.

● Your profile appears with the text styles applied to the `a.searchlink Small` class.

More Options!

You can generate interesting effects by changing how your Interests links appear when the user hovers the mouse pointer over them. Here's some example code for the `a.searchlinkSmall:hover` class:

```
a.searchlinkSmall:hover {font-size:12pt; color: Tomato;
font-weight: bold; text-decoration: none;}
```

You can make your profile much more attractive by changing the default font that MySpace uses for headings.

The right side of your profile contains sections titled Blurbs, Friend Space, and Friends Comments, and the Blurbs section has the subtitles About Me and Who I'd Like to Meet. These are your profile headings and they all appear in an ugly orange font.

To change the heading font to match the rest of your profile text, you need to apply the `font-family`, `font-size`, and `color` styles to the `.orangetext15` class.

① In MySpace, click Home.

② Click Edit Profile.

The Profile Edit - Interests & Personality page appears.

③ In the About Me text box, type the opening and closing `style` tags.

④ Type the styles for the `.orangetext15` class.

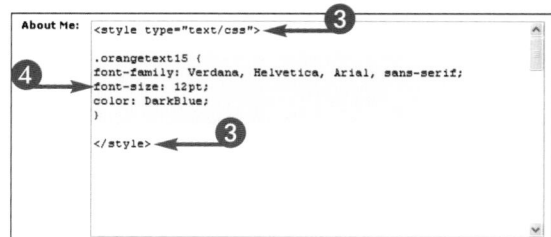

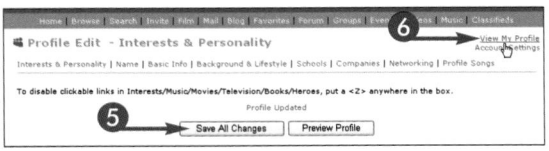

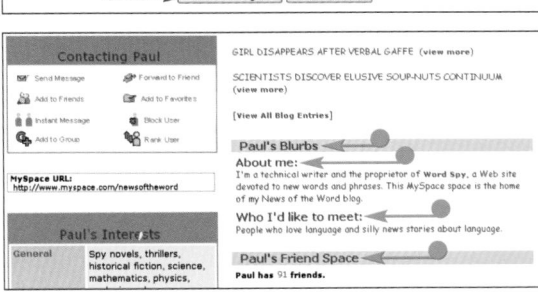

5 Click Save All Changes.

MySpace updates your profile.

6 Click View My Profile.

● Your profile appears with the text styles applied to the `.orangetext15` class.

More Options!

The right side of your profile includes two other headings: User's Latest Blog Entry and User Has *x* Friends. To customize this text to match the other headings, apply the `font-family`, `font-size`, and `color` styles to the `.btext` and `.redbtext` classes:

```
.btext,  .redbtext {font-family:Verdana,Helvetica,Arial,
sans-serif;font-size:12pt;  color: DarkBlue;}
```

You can integrate the MySpace navigation links into your profile by adjusting the link text to match your profile text.

The MySpace navigation bar is the strip of links that runs above your profile: Home, Browse, Search, and so on. By default, MySpace displays these links in a white font that turns black when you hover your mouse over a link. However, the white link text may become unreadable if you

change your background to white or another light color (as described in Chapter 3).

To change the navigation bar font to match the rest of your profile text, you need to apply the `font-family`, `font-size`, and `color` styles to the `a.navbar:link` and `a.navbar:hover` classes.

---

① In MySpace, click Home.

② Click Edit Profile.

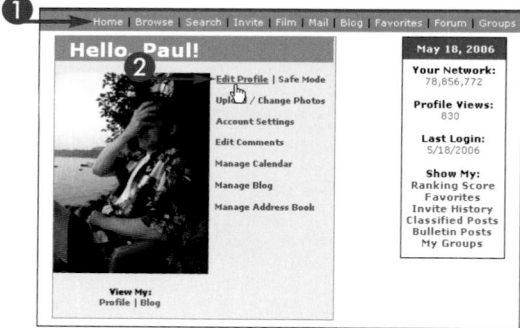

The Profile Edit - Interests & Personality page appears.

③ In the About Me text box, type the opening and closing `style` tags.

④ Type the styles for the `a.navbar:link` class.

⑤ Type the styles for the `a.navbar:hover` class.

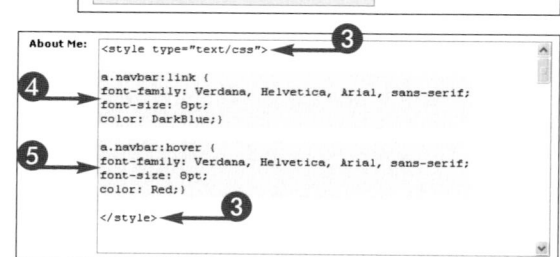

```
About Me:   <style type="text/css">

a.navbar:link {
font-family: Verdana, Helvetica, Arial, sans-serif;
font-size: 8pt;
color: DarkBlue;})

a.navbar:hover {
font-family: Verdana, Helvetica, Arial, sans-serif;
font-size: 8pt;
color: Red;})

</style>
```

Note: *Do not increase the size of the navigation bar links to more than 8 points. Otherwise, the navigation bar will wrap onto a second line for those readers running at a screen resolution of 800 x 600.*

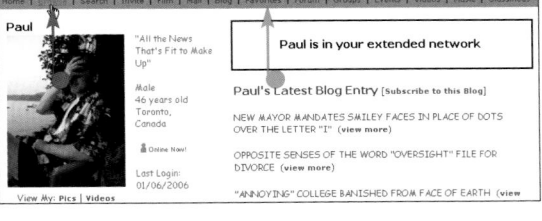

⑥ Click Save All Changes.

MySpace updates your profile.

⑦ Click View My Profile.

● Your profile appears with the text styles applied to the `a.navbar:link` class.

● Your profile appears with the text styles applied to the `a.navbar:hover` class.

More Options!

MySpace also displays several links in the footer that appears at the bottom of your profile. The footer text is controlled by the `a.text:link` class, but you may also want to remove the underlines that appear with the footer links. To do this, add the following code to a style block:

```
u {text-decoration:none;}
```

Change the Appearance of Your Link Text

You can improve the overall look of your profile by customizing the links that appear throughout the profile so that they match or complement the rest of the text.

Your MySpace profile has many links throughout: Pics and Videos under your profile picture; your schools; your Networking categories; Subscribe to This Blog; the View More text beside each blog entry; View All Blog Entries; the name of your friends; and the Add Comment text. By default, MySpace formats links as blue and bold, and this applies to any links you add to your own text.

To change the appearance of the link text, you need to apply the font-family, font-size, and color styles to the a and a:hover elements.

---

① In MySpace, click Home.

② Click Edit Profile.

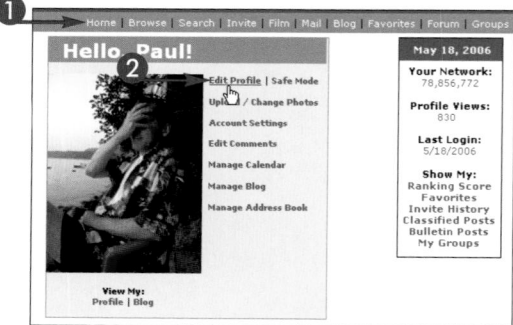

The Profile Edit - Interests & Personality page appears.

③ In the About Me text box, type the opening and closing style tags.

④ Type the styles for the a element.

⑤ Type the styles for the a:hover element.

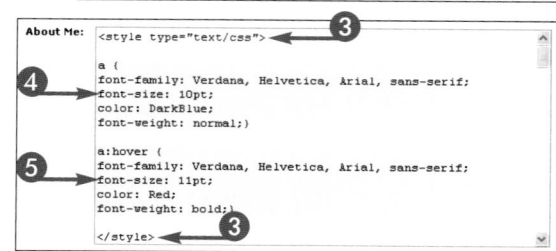

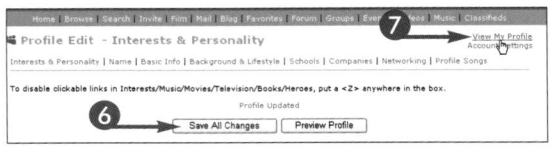

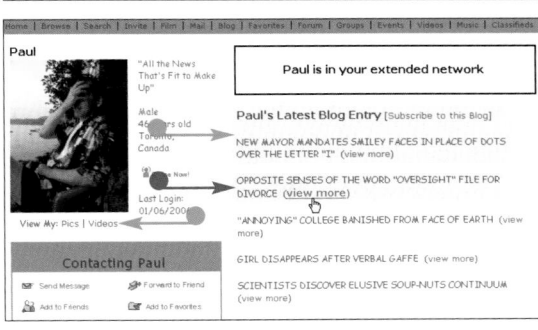

6 Click Save All Changes.

MySpace updates your profile.

7 Click View My Profile.

● Your profile appears with the text styles applied to the a element.

● Your profile appears with the text styles applied to the a:hover class.

More Options!

The only link in your profile that you have not yet seen how to customize is the View All of User's Friends link. To customize that, apply the font-family, font-size, and color styles to the a.redlink:link and a.redlink:hover classes.

Use Tags to Customize Your Text

You can add visual interest to parts of your profile by customizing text with HTML tags.

Your MySpace profile has two sections where you can type free-form text: About Me and Who I'd Like to Meet, both of which appear in the Blurbs module. You can customize words and phrases in this area by surrounding them with HTML tags. For example, to make a word bold,

surround it with the `<b>` and `</b>` tags. Similarly, you can make a word italic by surrounding it with `<i>` and `</i>` tags.

For more advanced customizing, surround the text with the `<span style>` and `</span>` tags. Set the `style` attribute equal to the style you want, as in this example that formats text as red:

`<span style="color: red">`

---

① In MySpace, click Home.

② Click Edit Profile.

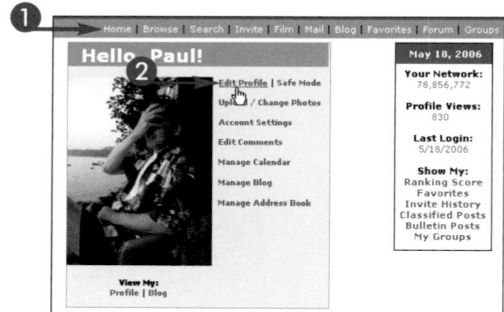

The Profile Edit - Interests & Personality page appears.

③ In the About Me text box, type your blurb and customize words and phrases with HTML tags.

④ In the I'd Like to Meet text box, type your blurb and customize words and phrases with HTML tags.

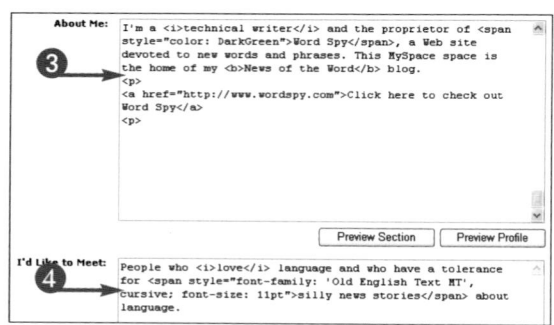

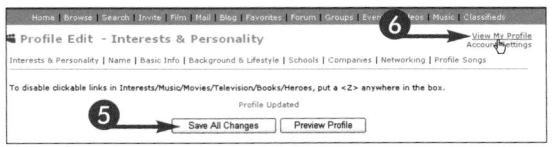

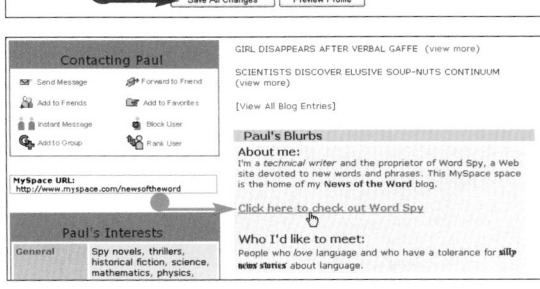

⑤ Click Save All Changes.

MySpace updates your profile.

⑥ Click View My Profile.

● Your profile appears with the customized text.

More Options!
To include a link in your blurbs, surround the link text with the
`<a hef="url">` and `</a>` tags. In the `<a hef="url">` tag, replace
`url` with the full address of the Web page, as in this example:

```
<a href="http://www.wordspy.com">
```

You can make your Interests or other lists of items more interesting by organizing them into Top 10 lists.

The Interests part of your MySpace profile contains lists for your favorite music, movies, television shows, books, and heroes. By default, MySpace displays these items as simple, comma-separated lists. However, you can use a bit of HTML to organize these items into

numbered lists, which enables you to convert your Interests into Top 10 lists.

To create a numbered list, begin with the `<ol>` tag and end with the `</ol>` tag. In between, for each item on the list, surround the item text with the `<li>` and `</li>` tags:

`<li>Gladiator</li>`

---

① In MySpace, click Home.

② Click Edit Profile.

The Profile Edit - Interests & Personality page appears.

③ In the section where you want your list to appear, type the `<ol>` tag.

④ For each item in the list, type `<li>`, the item text, and then `</li>`.

⑤ To complete the list, type the `</ol>` tag (not shown).

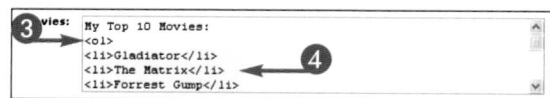

⑥ Click Save All Changes.

MySpace updates your profile.

⑦ Click View My Profile.

● Your profile appears with the Top 10 list.

Note: *After you organize items as a numbered list, MySpace no longer displays the items as links.*

More Options!
To apply a style to your numbered list text, you can add the style attribute to the `<li>` tag. However, this is too much work for long lists. Instead, apply a style to the li element using a style block in the About Me section:

```
li {font-family:Verdana,Helvetica,Arial,sans-serif;
font-size:10pt; color: DarkBlue;}
```

You can make your Interests or other lists of items more visually appealing by displaying them as bulleted lists.

The default lists for your interests, favorite music, movies, television shows, books, and heroes run across each module, from left to right, separated by commas. If you have a long list, this layout can make the items difficult to read. However, you can use some HTML to organize these items into bulleted lists.

To create a bulleted list, begin with the `<ul>` tag and end with the `</ul>` tag. In between, for each item on the list, surround the item text with the `<li>` and `</li>` tags:

`<li>Black Dogs</li>`

---

① In MySpace, click Home.

② Click Edit Profile.

The Profile Edit - Interests & Personality page appears.

③ In the section where you want your list to appear, type the `<ul>` tag.

④ For each item in the list, type `<li>`, the item text, and then `</li>`.

⑤ To complete the list, type the `</ul>` tag (not shown).

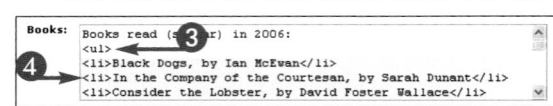

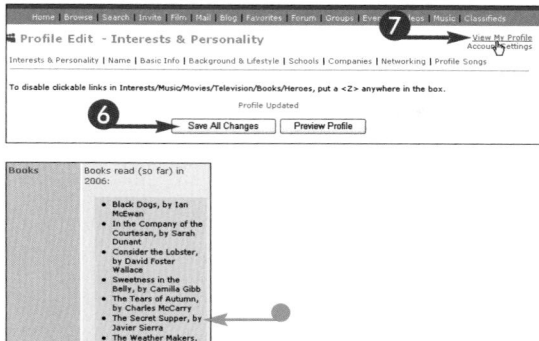

⑥ Click Save All Changes.

MySpace updates your profile.

⑦ Click View My Profile.

● Your profile appears with the bulleted list.

Note: *After you organize items as a bulleted list, MySpace no longer displays the items as links.*

More Options!
The default bulleted list uses a small black dot as the bullet. If you want a different bullet style, add the `type` attribute to the `<ul>` tag. Set `type` to `circle` for a circular bullet:

`<ul type="circle">`

You can also set `type` to `square` for a square bullet:

`<ul type="square">`

Include a Scrolling Text Marquee

You can add an eye-catching animation effect to your profile by creating a marquee that scrolls text across the screen.

Your profile text is usually static on the screen, which is probably the way you want it most of the time. However, most Web page designers know that the subtle use of animated effects can bring life to a page. These effects are normally created using JavaScript, but MySpace does not allow you to embed scripts in your profile.

To work around this limitation, you can insert text between the `<marquee>` and `</marquee>` tags:

`<marquee>Text</marquee>`

This text will then enter the module on the right, scroll all the way across the module, exit the module, and repeat.

---

① In MySpace, click Home.

② Click Edit Profile.

The Profile Edit - Interests & Personality page appears.

③ In the section where you want your scrolling text to appear, type the `<marquee>` tag.

④ Type the text that you want to scroll.

⑤ To complete the marquee, type the `</marquee>` tag.

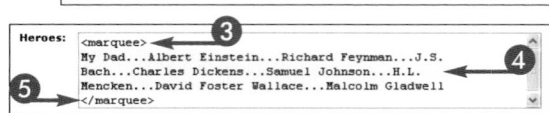

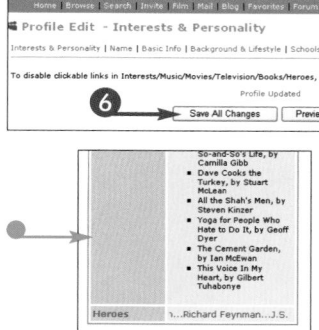

6 Click Save All Changes.

MySpace updates your profile.

7 Click View My Profile.

● Your profile appears with the scrolling text.

TIP

More Options!
There are several attributes you can use to customize the `<marquee>` tag. For example, if you want the text to scroll only a certain number of times, add the `loop` attribute and set it to the number of times you want the text to scroll. If you want the text to scroll in and stop on the left, add the `behavior` attribute and set it to `slide`. To scroll in the opposite direction, set the `direction` attribute to `right`:

```
<marquee loop="3" behavior="slide" direction="right">
```

Customizing Your Profile Layout

The default layout of your MySpace profile is serviceable, but very plain and not all that attractive. If you want to get noticed on MySpace and impress all your friends, then you need to customize the layout to suit your personal tastes and style.

Although MySpace gives you no direct method for customizing your layout, you can perform all kinds of fun and interesting tricks using HTML tags and Cascading Style Sheets (CSS) code. For example, you can change the background from the default

white to some other color or to an image of your choice. You can jazz up your profile with a banner and replace your profile name and the "extended network" box with custom images. You can even replace the unattractive Contact table with something much nicer. If you want to learn more about HTML and CSS, see *HTML: Your visual blueprint for designing effective Web pages with HTML, CSS, and XHTML*, by Paul Whitehead.

Quick Tips

Display a Background Image

You can spruce up your profile by changing the background to an image. The default profile background is white, which makes it easy to read your text, but it is not very interesting. For more visual appeal, you can customize the background to display an image of your choice. You do this by adding a style sheet to your profile and applying the `background-image` style to the `body` element using the following syntax:

```
body {
background-image: url(address);
background-repeat: value;
}
```

Here, change *address* to the address of the image on the Web. For the `background-repeat` *value*, use `repeat` to have the image tiled to cover the entire background, or `no-repeat` to use a single image only.

---

① In MySpace, click Home.

② Click Edit Profile.

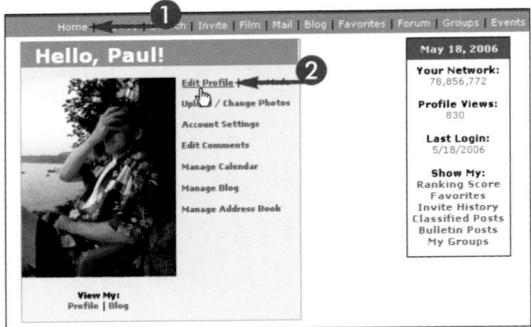

The Profile Edit - Interests & Personality page appears.

③ In the About Me text box, type the opening and closing `style` tags.

④ Type the CSS code for the image you want to use as the background.

⑤ Add `background-color: transparent` for the `table` and `td` elements.

Note: *You need to set the background color to transparent to enable the background image to show through.*

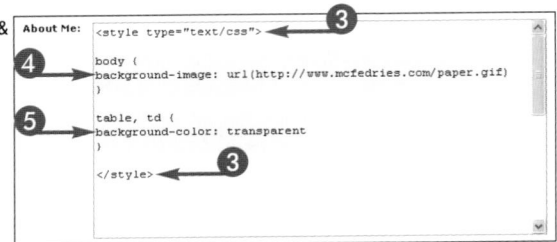

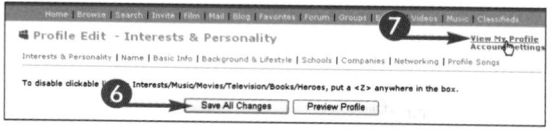

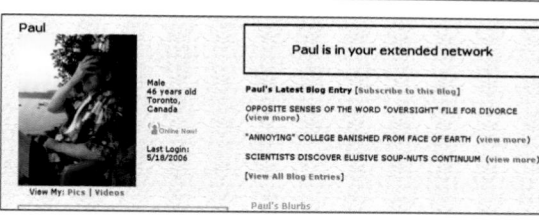

Note: *When choosing your background, be careful which image you choose. If the background is too dark or too "busy," your text may be unreadable.*

⑥ Click Save All Changes.

MySpace updates your profile.

⑦ Click View My Profile.

Your profile appears with the image in the background.

More Options!

If you would rather change the background color instead of using an image, replace the `background-image` style with `background-color` and specify the color you want. For example, the following style sets the background to teal:

```
background-color: teal;
```

If your MySpace profile has a particular title or theme, you can better display that title or theme by placing a banner image at the top of the profile.

The default MySpace profile "announces" your site by placing your name in a box above your profile image. If you want to project a stronger or flashier image, you can add a banner image to the top of the profile.

The banner image should be 800 pixels wide (the width of your profile), but the height can be whatever you need for your image, text, logo, or whatever. You add the image to your profile by creating a CSS class that specifies various image properties, including the `width`, `height`, `position`, and `background-image`. You then insert a `div` tag that uses the `class` attribute to reference the image.

① In MySpace, click Home.

② Click Edit Profile.

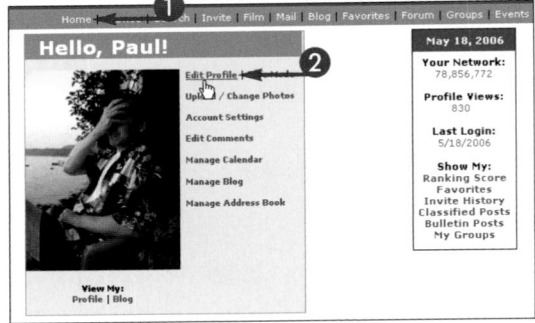

The Profile Edit - Interests & Personality page appears.

③ In the About Me text box, type a `div` tag that references your `banner` class (see Step **5**).

④ Type the opening and closing `style` tags.

⑤ Type the CSS code for the `banner` class.

⑥ Add code to reset the profile margins.

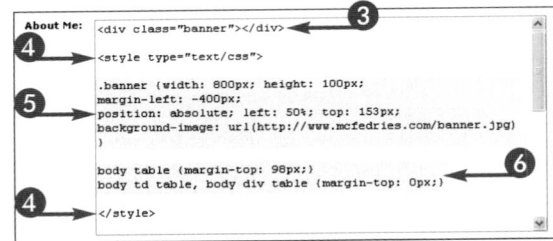

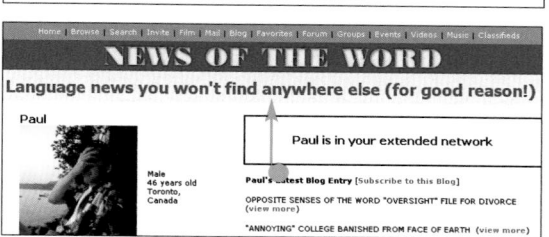

⑦ Click Save All Changes.

MySpace updates your profile.

⑧ Click View My Profile.

● Your banner appears at the top of the profile.

Important!

In the class definition for the banner, be sure to change the `height` property to the height of your image. Also, you may need to play with the value of the `top` property to ensure the banner appears just below the navigation bar. For the `body table` element, you may need to adjust the `margin-top` value to ensure there is no gap between your banner and the top of your profile.

You can add visual interest to your profile by replacing the simple text that MySpace uses to display your profile name with a custom image that you create.

You can spruce up your profile by replacing your profile name with an attractive image. You do that by taking advantage of the fact that MySpace defines a special CSS class for your profile name: `.nametext`. This class enables

you to manipulate any CSS style for that section of the profile, including the `background-image` style. Again, you use this style to specify the image you want to use. You also need to specify the `height` and `width` of the image and set the `background-repeat` style to `no-repeat`. You also need to hide the name text by setting the `font-size` to 0.

---

① In MySpace, click Home.

② Click Edit Profile.

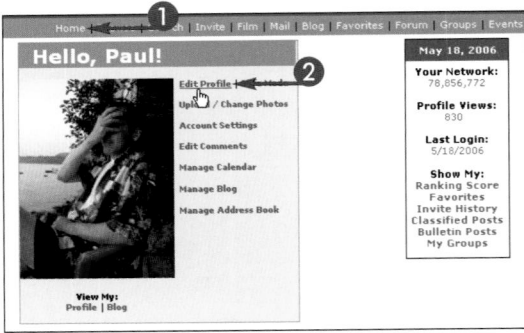

The Profile Edit - Interests & Personality page appears.

③ Type the opening and closing `style` tags.

④ Type the CSS code for the `.nametext` class.

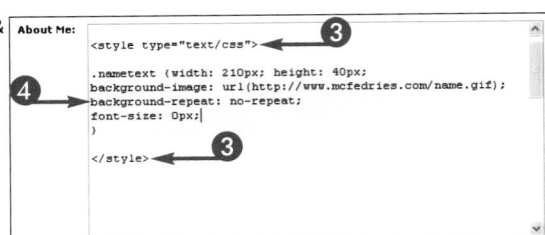

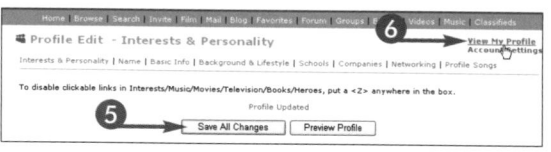

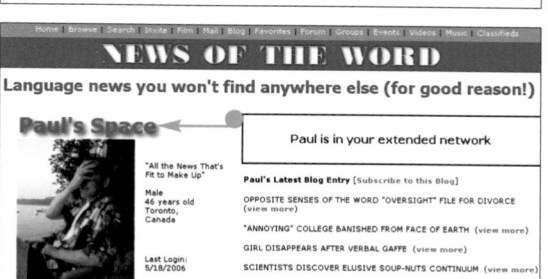

⑤ Click Save All Changes.

MySpace updates your profile.

⑥ Click View My Profile.

● Your image appears in place of your profile name.

Caution!
The only downside to hiding your profile name text is that it also means you hide your away message, if you have one (see the "Set Up a Message to Display When You Are Offline" task in Chapter 1). If it is important to you to display your away message, do not hide your profile name.

You can improve the look of your profile by replacing the default Contact table with your own custom version.

The default Contact table MySpace provides is not exactly eye catching, so a lot of MySpace members replace it with their own creation. Use a graphics program to create a 300×150 image, and add your own link text.

You work with the Contact table using a special CSS class named `.contactTable`, and you use it to set (among others) the

`width`, `height`, and `background-image` styles:

```
.contactTable {
width:300px !important;
height:150px !important;
background-image:url(address);}
```

You also have to hide the default MySpace Contact table:

```
.contactTable table,
table.contactTable td {
background-image:none; }
.contactTable a img
{visibility: hidden;}
```

---

① In MySpace, click Home.

② Click Edit Profile.

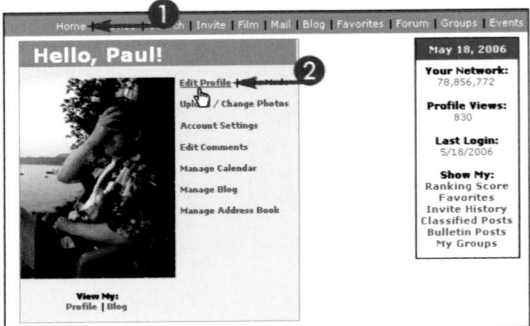

The Profile Edit - Interests & Personality page appears.

③ Type the opening and closing `style` tags.

④ Type the CSS code for the `.contactTable` class.

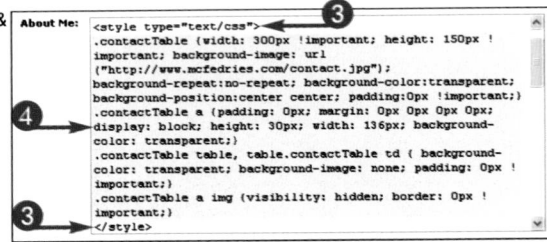

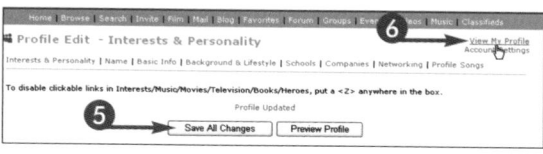

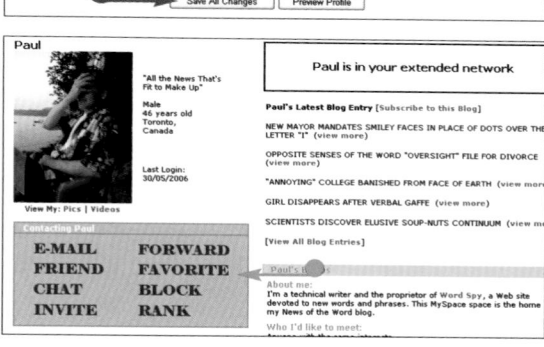

⑤ Click Save All Changes.

MySpace updates your profile.

⑥ Click View My Profile.

● Your Contact table appears.

Check This Out!

If you do not want to create your own Contact table image, there are many sites on the Web that offer free images that you can use. Run a Google search on the phrase "contact tables" and you will get a lot of results to check out.

You can make your page look neater by tweaking the MySpace tables to give them a consistent appearance.

The MySpace layout is a series of nested tables. By applying the same styles to these tables, you can create a consistent layout that looks much neater than the default layout. You need to tweak the following table elements:

```
table, tr, td,
table table
table table td
table table table
```

```
table table table td
table table table table
table table table table td
```

In each case, you set consistent properties for the `background-color`, `margin`, `padding`, and anything else you want to adjust. You also need to adjust the width of two classes: `.whitetext12` (module headings) and `.nametext`, as well as the URL box:

```
table tr td table tr td table tr
td div
```

---

1 In MySpace, click Home.

2 Click Edit Profile.

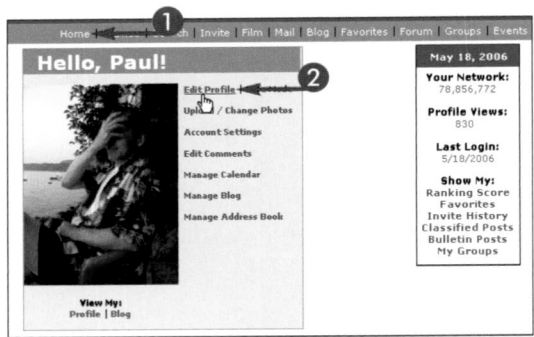

The Profile Edit - Interests & Personality page appears.

3 Type the opening and closing `style` tags.

4 Type the CSS code for the table elements.

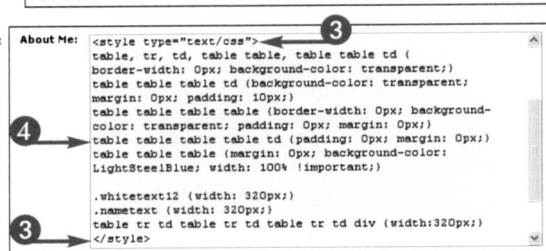

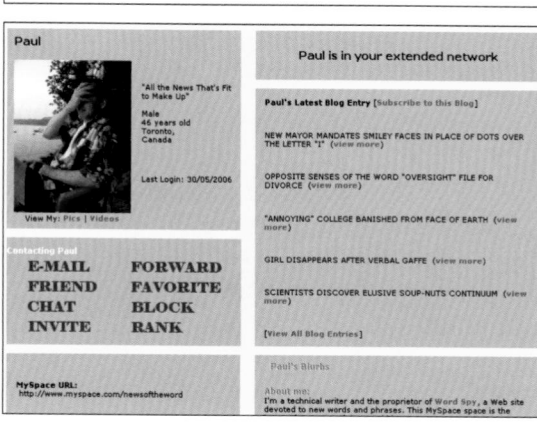

5 Click Save All Changes.

MySpace updates your profile.

6 Click View My Profile.

Your MySpace profile appears with a consistent table layout.

Try This!

For some interesting profile effects, try adjusting the background-color style for different table elements. Alternatively, if you want your layout to appear without any obvious tables at all, set the background-color style for each table element to transparent.

You can add some visual appeal to your profile by adding borders around the various modules.

MySpace profile tables often look best if they have a border around them. You can add borders by modifying the following profile element:

`table table table`

In particular, you can modify three border styles: `border-width`, `border-color`, and `border-style`.

For `border-style`, you can apply six different effects: `double`, `groove`, `inset`, `outset`, `ridge`, and `solid`. For example, the following code gives you 5-pixel, dark blue, double borders:

```
table table table {
border-width: 5px;
border-color: DarkBlue;
border-style: double; }
```

① In MySpace, click Home.

② Click Edit Profile.

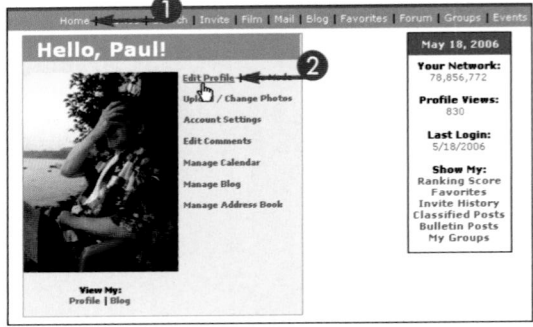

The Profile Edit - Interests & Personality page appears.

③ Type the opening and closing `style` tags.

④ Type the CSS code for the table elements.

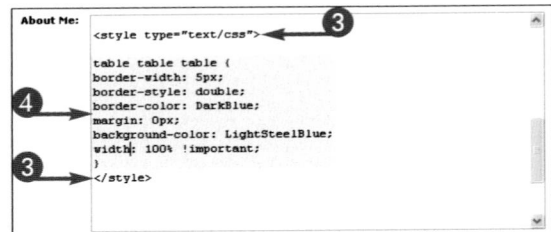

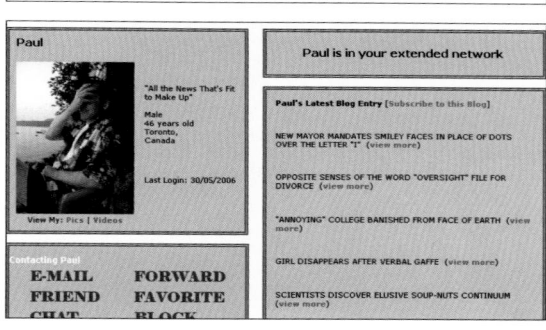

5 Click Save All Changes.

MySpace updates your profile.

6 Click View My Profile.

Your MySpace profile appears with borders around the modules.

Try This!

To reduce the amount of CSS code you have to write, you can use a shorthand notation that applies the `border-width`, `border-style`, and `border-color` styles in a single line:

`border: width style color;`

For example, the following style sets the borders to 3 pixels, solid, and gold:

`border: 3px solid Gold`

You can enhance the look of your profile modules by separating each module's title and text with a border.

The various module titles — Contacting User, User's Interests, User's Details, and so on, are controlled by the `.whitetext12` class. You learned more about this class in Chapter 2. For now, you can use this class to add a border that separates the module title

from the module text. You do this by applying the `border-bottom-width`, `border-bottom-style`, and `border-bottom-color` styles, which take the same values as `border-width`, `border-color`, and `border-style` described in the previous task. You can also place a border under your profile name by modifying the `.nametext` class.

---

① In MySpace, click Home.

② Click Edit Profile.

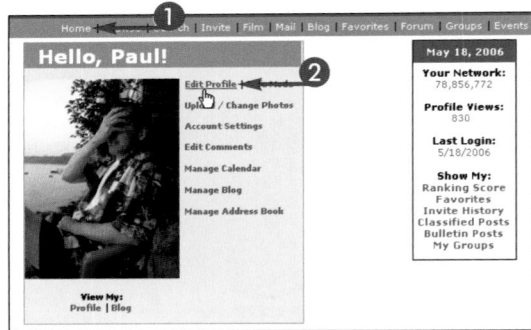

The Profile Edit - Interests & Personality page appears.

③ Type the opening and closing `style` tags.

④ Type the CSS code for the borders.

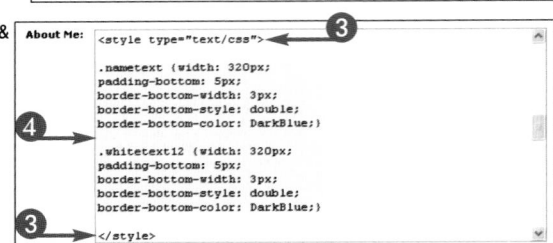

⑤ Click Save All Changes.

MySpace updates your profile.

⑥ Click View My Profile.

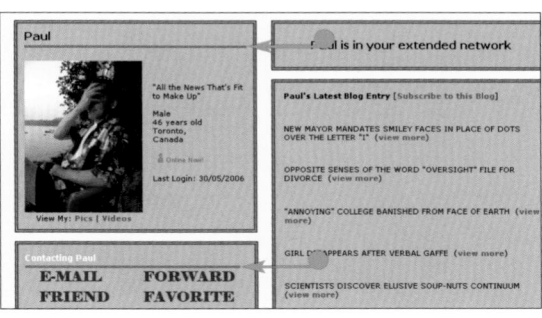

● Your MySpace profile appears with borders below the module titles.

Try This!

You can reduce the amount of CSS code you have to write by using a shorthand notation that applies the `border-bottom-width`, `border-bottom-style`, and `border-bottom-color` styles in a single line:

`border-bottom: width style color;`

For example, the following style sets the borders to 5 pixels, outset, and orange:

`border-bottom: 5px outset Orange`

You can make better use of the Extended Network box by replacing it with a custom image.

In the default profile setup, the top of the right column is home to the Extended Network box, which tells visitors that you are in their extended MySpace network. This is meaningless (*every* MySpace member is in your extended network), so you can make better use of the space by replacing it with an image of your choice, which can be a picture, logo, or formatted text.

You do that by taking advantage of the fact that MySpace defines a special CSS class for the Extended Network box: .blacktext12. This class enables you to manipulate any CSS style for that section of the profile, including the background-image style, which you set to the URL of your image. An image approximately 300 pixels wide and 50 pixels high will fit comfortably in the Extended Network box.

---

1 In MySpace, click Home.

2 Click Edit Profile.

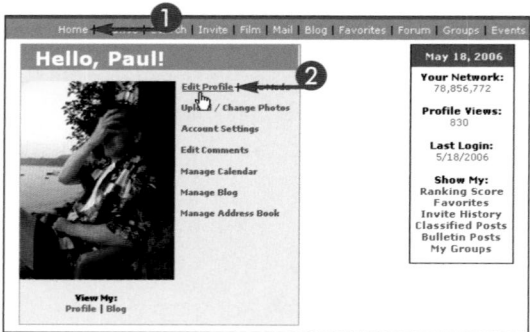

The Profile Edit - Interests & Personality page appears.

3 Type the opening and closing style tags.

4 Type the CSS code for the .blacktext12 class.

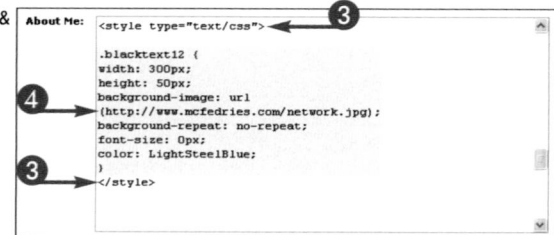

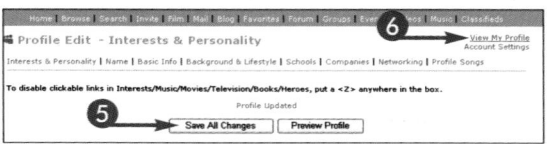

⑤ Click Save All Changes.

MySpace updates your profile.

⑥ Click View My Profile.

● Your MySpace profile appears with your image in the Extended Network box.

More Options!
Do not forget that you also need to hide the Extended Network box text. You do this by modifying two styles of the `.blacktext12` class: You set the `font-size` to 0, and you set the `color` to the same color as the `background-color` style.

65

If you do not want other people to see who your friends are or to read your friends' comments, you can hide those parts of your profile.

Most MySpace members like to make as many friends as they can, and some even think that your "status" on MySpace is determined by the number of friends you have. If you are on MySpace for the music or to run your blog, then you may not care about your Friends list or about showing comments from friends. In that case, you can hide those parts of your profile by adding the following code to the end of your I'd Like to Meet section:

```
<div style="display: none;
visibility: hidden;">
<table><tr><td>
<table><tr><td>
```

① In MySpace, click Home.

② Click Edit Profile.

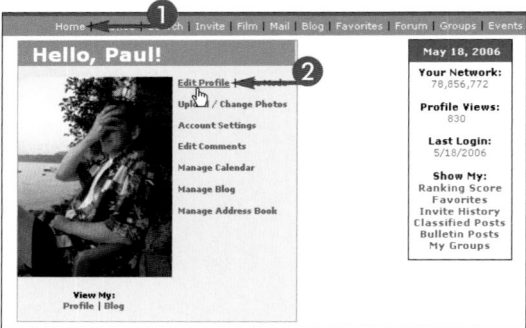

The Profile Edit - Interests & Personality page appears.

③ At the end of the I'd Like to Meet section, type the code for hiding the friends and comments.

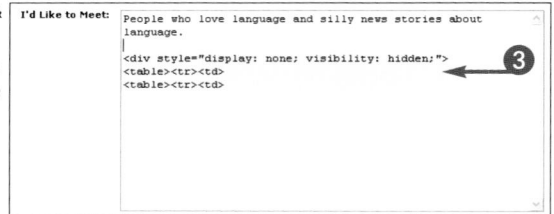

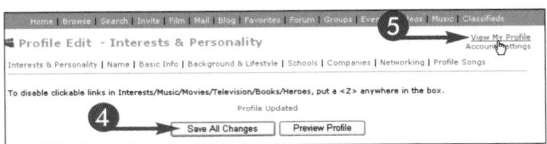

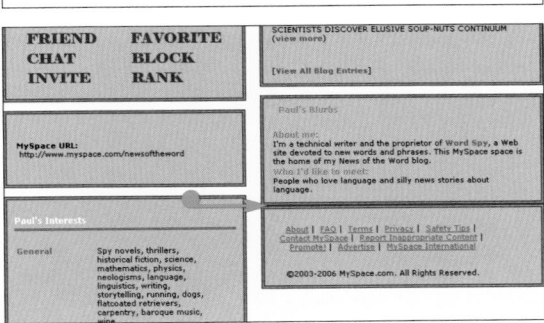

④ Click Save All Changes.

MySpace updates your profile.

⑤ Click View My Profile.

● Your MySpace profile appears with your friends and comments hidden.

More Options!
If you want to hide your Contact box, add the following code to a style block in the About Me section:

```
.contactTable {display: none; visibility: hidden;}
```

Communicating with MySpace

MySpace is one of the most popular and most famous communities on the Web. Communities in the real world thrive on the interaction between their members, whether it is conversation, getting together, making calls, writing letters, and so on.

MySpace is no different. It is much more than a collection of personal profiles and blogs because it gives you many different ways to interact with fellow MySpace members. You can post bulletins, send invitations, receive text messages, join a group, create your own group, post a classified ad, and much more.

Quick Tips

You can send a quick message to everyone in your MySpace Friends list by posting a bulletin.

By definition, the people on your MySpace Friends list are people who want to hear from you. If you have something interesting happening in your life, your Friends want to hear about it. It does not matter if you have recently graduated, received a promotion, moved, or declared a new favorite color.

Whatever the news, you can quickly broadcast it to all the people in your Friends list by posting a *bulletin*, a short message that MySpace distributes automatically to all your Friends.

---

① Click Home.

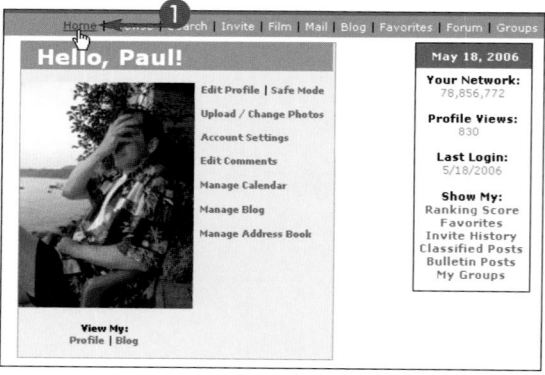

② In the My Mail section, click Post Bulletin.

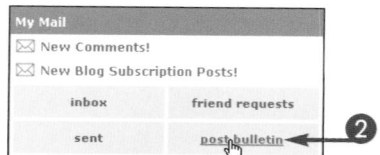

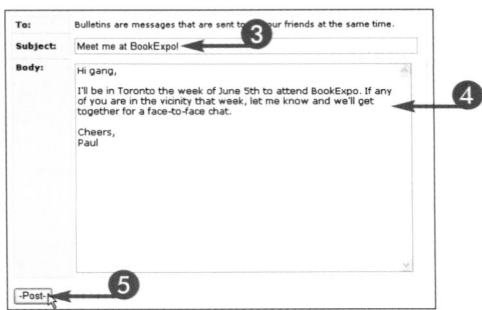

The Post Bulletin page appears.

3 Use the Subject text box any to type a subject for the bulletin.

4 Use the Body text box to type the bulletin message.

5 Click Post.

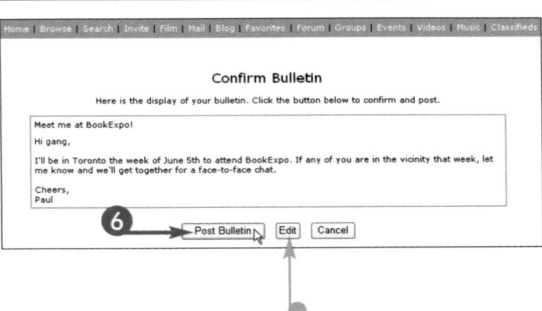

The Confirm Bulletin page appears.

● If you notice a mistake in your bulletin, click Edit to return to the Post Bulletin page.

6 Click Post Bulletin.

MySpace sends the bulletin to your friends.

More Options!

You can also post a bulletin via the MySpace Mail Center. In the navigation bar, click Mail to display the Mail Center. Click Bulletin to display your Bulletin Board, which shows the bulletins your friends have sent. Click Post Bulletin and then follow Steps **3** to **6**. Note, too, that when you display the Bulletin Board page, you can see the bulletins you have sent by clicking the Show Bulletins I've Posted link.

Send a MySpace Invitation

You can easily add people you know to your MySpace Friends list by sending those people an invitation to join MySpace.

MySpace is a great way to meet new people. Often it is a simple matter of clicking an interest, checking out the members who share that interest, and then sending a Friend request.

However, just like in the real world, MySpace can seem more fun and more comfortable if you have a few familiar faces around. If your real-world friends and family are not yet on MySpace, you can send them a MySpace e-card that includes a link for joining MySpace.

---

① Click Invite.

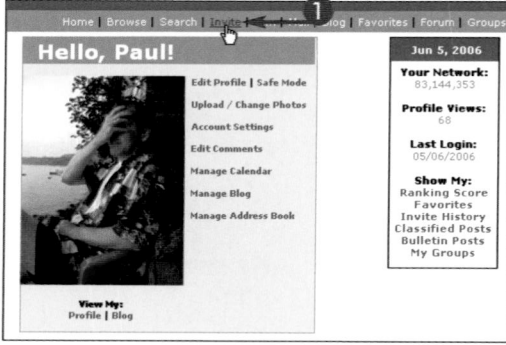

The Invite Your Friends to MySpace page appears.

② Use the To text box to type the e-mail address of the person you want to invite.

Note: *To invite multiple people at once, separate each e-mail address with a comma.*

③ Use the Your Message Here text box to type a message that appears above the MySpace link.

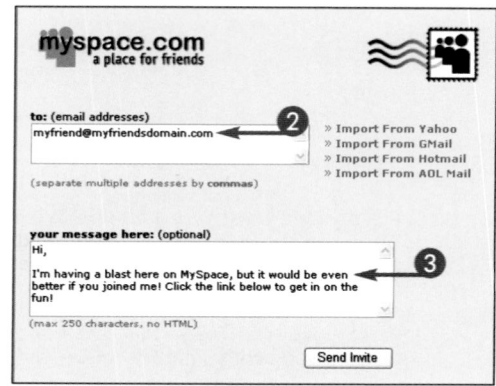

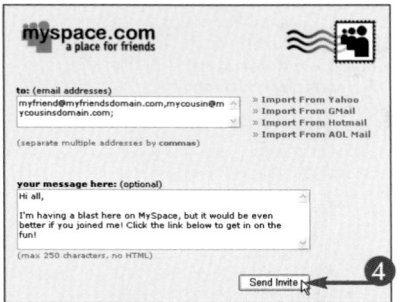

④ Click Send Invite.

MySpace sends the invitation and displays the Invite History page.

More Options!
You can use the Invite History page to work with your previous invitations. To see this page without sending an invite, click Invite and then click the View Past Invites link. To resend an invitation, click the corresponding Remind link in the Action column. To remind all your pending invites, make sure each Remind column check box is activated (☐ changes to ☑), and then click the Remind button. If you give up on someone, click the corresponding Delete link in the Action column.

You can send a MySpace invitation using a regular e-mail message and have MySpace automatically insert your Invite link into that message.

When you send an invitation to join MySpace using a MySpace e-card, the From line of the message shows as "*User* at MySpace," where *User* is your MySpace profile name. If you are using a MySpace profile name that the recipient may not recognize, then that person may delete the message without reading your invitation. To avoid that, you might prefer to send the invitation using your regular e-mail program. That way, the recipient sees your name on the message. To make this easier, MySpace can insert your Invite link automatically into a new e-mail message.

---

① Click Invite.

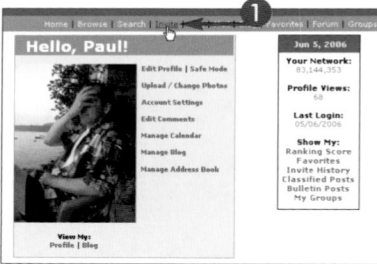

The Invite Your Friends to MySpace page appears.

② Click Show My Invite Link.

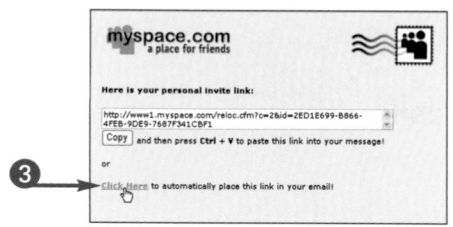

MySpace displays your Invite link.

③ Click the Click Here link.

A new mail message appears with the link inserted.

④ Type the address of the person you want to invite.

⑤ Click your e-mail program's Send option to send the message.

Important!
This task does not work with Web-based e-mail services such as MSN Hotmail, Google Gmail, or Yahoo! Mail. You need to run this task using a computer that has an e-mail program such as Outlook, Windows Mail, or Mac OSX Mail. Note, too, that MySpace creates the new message using whatever program is set up as the default mail client on your computer.

Import Friends and Invitation Addresses

You can quickly send a message to multiple people by creating a contact list in your MySpace Address Book.

After you add a MySpace member as a contact in your Address Book, you can send that person a message by clicking the envelope icon that appears in the MySpace Profile column. If you want to send the

same message to multiple people, it takes too long to do it one person at a time. A faster method is to create a contact list that includes some or all of your contacts. When you send a message to the contact list, all the people on the list receive the message.

---

① Click Invite.

② Click the link for the service from which you want to import the addresses.

MySpace prompts you to enter your login information.

③ Type your login ID.

④ Type your password.

⑤ Click Get Contacts.

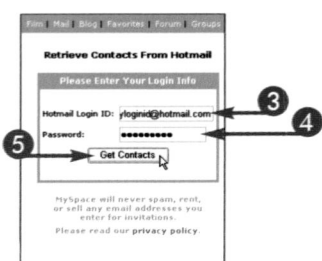

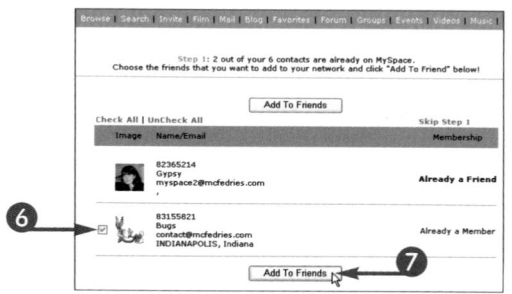

MySpace displays a list of contacts who are MySpace members.

⑥ If there are any contacts that you do not want to add as a friend, click the check box (☑ changes to ☐).

Note: *MySpace members not already on your Friends list have their check boxes activated by default. Be sure to uncheck any contacts that you do not want to add as a friend.*

⑦ Click Add To Friends.

MySpace displays a list of contacts who are not MySpace members.

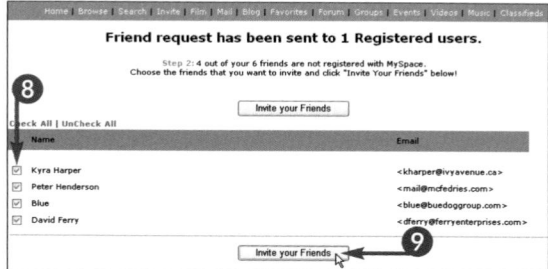

⑧ For each contact that you do not want to invite to MySpace, click the check box (☑ changes to ☐).

Note: *Contacts who are not MySpace members have their check boxes activated by default. Uncheck any contacts that you do not want to invite to MySpace.*

⑨ Click Invite Your Friends.

MySpace sends invitation messages to each contact.

More Options!

You can also invite people to join MySpace by adding them to your MySpace Address Book (see the "Add a Contact to Your Address Book" task later in this chapter). Click Mail and then click Address Book to display your contacts. In the MySpace Profile column, click the Invite link next to the contact's name.

Receive a Text Message for MySpace Alerts

You can keep on top of what is happening with your MySpace profile by arranging to have alerts sent as text messages to your mobile phone.

In the MySpace world, an *alert* is a message that tells you about activity on your MySpace profile. There are six main types of alerts: friend requests, blog comments, profile comments, image comments, new messages, and event invitations.

If you will be away from a computer for a while, then you might miss some important alerts. To ensure you are always aware of what is going on with your profile, you can configure MySpace to send alerts as text messages to your mobile phone.

---

① In MySpace, click Home.

② Click Account Settings.

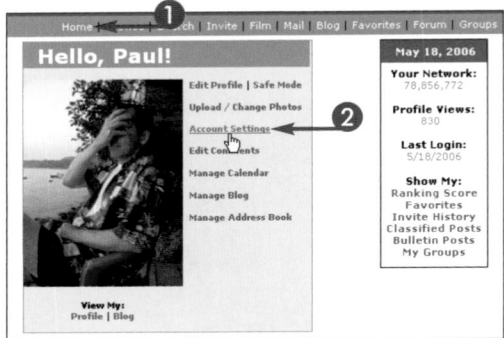

The Change Account Settings window appears.

③ Next to Mobile Settings, click Change Settings.

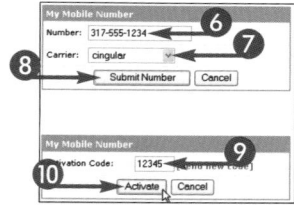

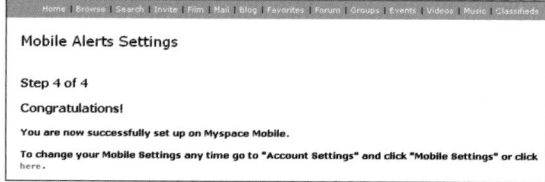

The Mobile Alerts Settings window appears.

④ Click the check box for each alert type you do not want to receive (☑ changes to ☐).

Note: All the alerts have their check boxes activated by default. Be sure to uncheck any alerts that you do not want to receive.

⑤ Click Apply Settings.

MySpace displays the My Mobile Number controls.

⑥ Type your mobile phone number.

⑦ Use the Carrier list to select your mobile provider.

⑧ Click Submit Number.

MySpace sends you a text message with your Activation Code.

⑨ Type your Activation Code.

⑩ Click Activate.

MySpace sends alerts to your mobile phone.

Reverse It!
If you no longer want to receive alerts as text messages, MySpace gives you two ways to stop them. The first method is to follow Steps **1** to **3** to display the Mobile Alerts Settings page, and then click the Disable link in the My Mobile Number section. The second method is to text the word STOP to the short code MYSPC.

With the Address Book, you can use MySpace to store data such as e-mail addresses and phone numbers of people you know.

If you use MySpace frequently, you can have the contact data for people you know at your fingertips by adding those people to your MySpace Address Book. The Address Book enables you to store names, MySpace usernames, up to three e-mail addresses, up to three phone numbers, and up to three instant messaging screen names. You can also add notes for each contact, which enables you to record birthdays, anniversaries, and other things you want to remember. The Address Book also provides links so that you can quickly send messages to your contacts.

---

① **Click Mail.**

The Mail Center page appears.

② **Click Address Book.**

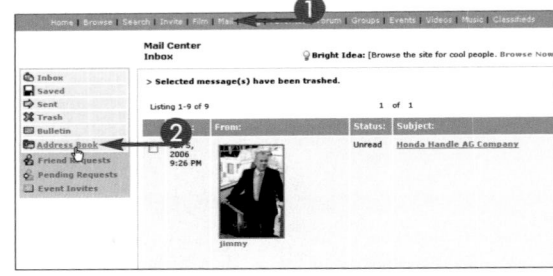

The Address Book page appears.

③ **Click Add a Contact.**

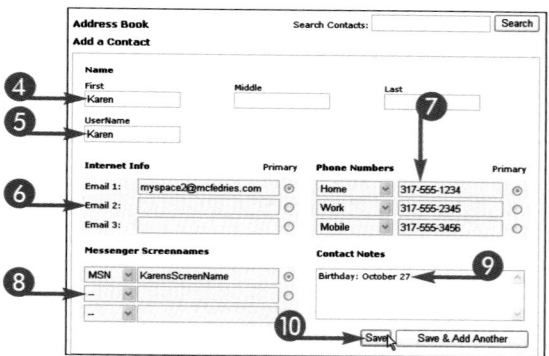

The Add a Contact page appears.

④ Type the person's name.

⑤ If the person is a MySpace member, type the person's username (profile name).

⑥ Type one or more e-mail addresses.

⑦ Type one or more phone numbers.

⑧ Type one or more instant messaging screen names.

⑨ Type some notes.

⑩ Click Save.

● MySpace adds the contact to your Address Book.

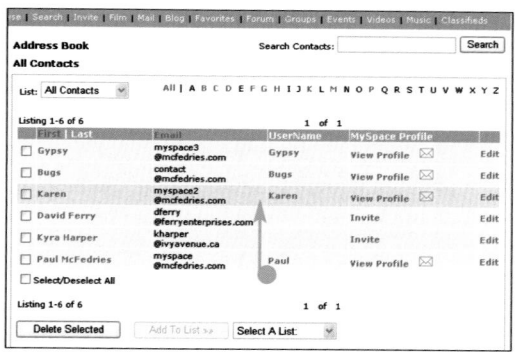

More Options!

MySpace gives you a quicker method to add a contact if you just want to enter basic information. Follow Steps **1** and **2** to display the Address Book page. Below the address list you see a Quick Add Contact section. Type a First Name, Last Name, Primary Email address, and MySpace UserName, and then click Add.

Join a Group

You can join a MySpace group and converse with other members on a topic that interests you.

One of the most impressive resources in all of MySpace is the Groups feature. A *group* is a forum devoted to a particular subject. Group members post messages to the group, other members respond to those messages, and so on. Most groups are

home to many such conversations. What makes the Groups feature so impressive is that there are over two *million* groups available, so you are bound to find a group for any topic that interests you.

Although you can view a group and its recent messages without joining, if you want to post messages and pictures, then you must join the group.

---

① Click Groups.

② Click the category that contains the group you want to join.

● You can also type a word or two in the Keywords text box and then click Search.

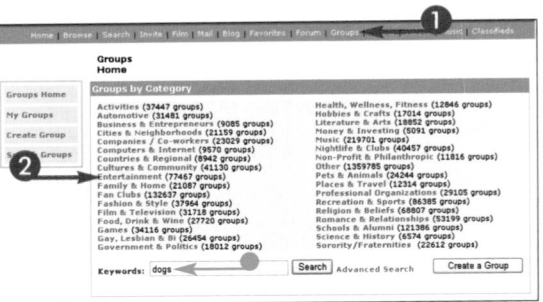

MySpace displays a list of groups.

③ Scroll through the list until you find the group you want or a group that looks interesting.

④ To view information about the group, click the group title.

● If you are sure you want to join the group, click the Join link, instead, and skip to Step **6**.

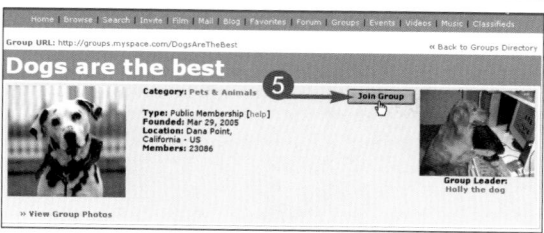

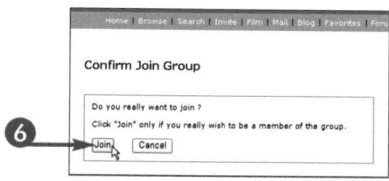

MySpace displays the group's profile.

Note: *It is a good idea to examine the information on the group's profile, which also includes recent posts to the group. This will give you a good idea whether you will enjoy the group.*

⑤ To join this group, click Join Group.

MySpace asks you to confirm.

⑥ Click Join.

MySpace adds you as a member of the group.

Note: *If the group is private, your request is sent to the group moderator, who will then either accept or deny your request to join.*

More Options!

After you join a group or two, click Groups and then click My Groups to see the list of groups to which you belong. Click a group to load its profile. As a member, you now see a number of buttons, including Post Topic (to post a new message to the group), Upload Image (to add an image to the group's archive), and Post Bulletin (to post a bulletin to all group members that accept them — see the next task).

You can configure your settings for a group so that you receive bulletins sent by the group moderator or by group members.

The profile page of a group includes a Post Bulletin button that enables the group moderator or a group member to send a bulletin to every member of the group. (If you do not see the Post Bulletin button, it means that the moderator has turned off this feature.) However, receiving group bulletins is an "opt-in" feature, which means you have to configure your group settings to receive bulletins. You can elect to receive bulletins from the moderator, from members, or from both.

① Click Groups.

② Click My Groups.

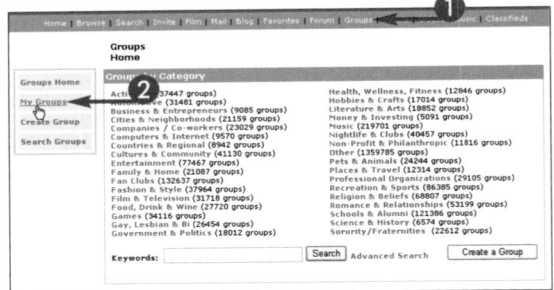

MySpace displays a list of the groups you have joined.

③ Click the group from which you want to receive bulletins.

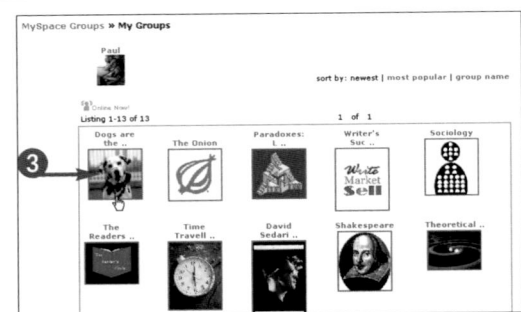

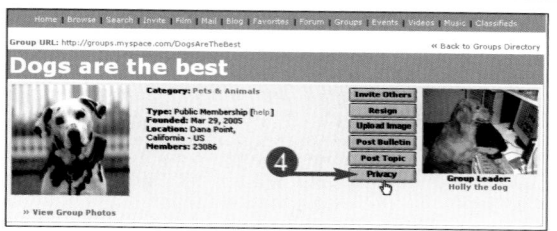

MySpace displays the
group's profile.

④ Click Privacy.

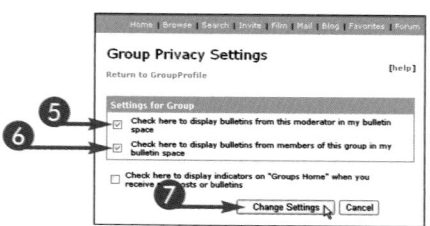

The Group Privacy
Settings page appears.

⑤ Click here to receive
bulletins from the
group moderator
(☐ changes to ☑).

⑥ Click here to receive
bulletins from the
group members
(☐ changes to ☑).

⑦ Click Change Settings.

MySpace updates the
group settings and you
will now receive bulletins
from all your groups.

More Options!
To make sure you do not miss any group posts, you can configure
MySpace to indicate on the Groups home page when any of your
groups have new posts. Follow Steps **1** to **4**, click Check Here to
Display Indicators on "Groups Home" When You Receive New Posts
or Bulletins (☐ changes to ☑), and then click Change Settings.

Resign from a Group

If you no longer enjoy a group, you can resign from it to prevent it from cluttering the My Groups page.

With more than two million groups available, it is a certainty that some groups will be better than others. Most group moderators try to keep the discussions civil and focused on the group topic, but many do not succeed. As a result, such groups are riddled with rude or obnoxious members, off-topic posts, and spam. (Note that this is much less of a problem in private groups.) Fortunately, MySpace makes it easy to resign from a group that you no longer like. This not only reduces clutter in the My Groups page, but it also prevents group members from viewing your profile.

① Click Groups.

② Click My Groups.

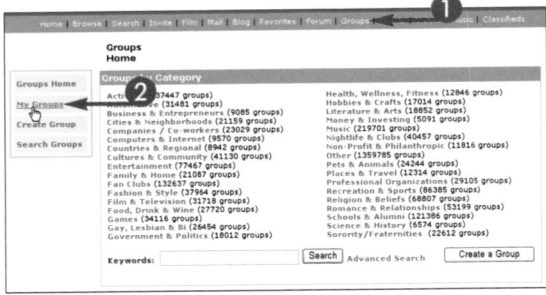

MySpace displays a list of the groups you have joined.

③ Click the group you want to leave.

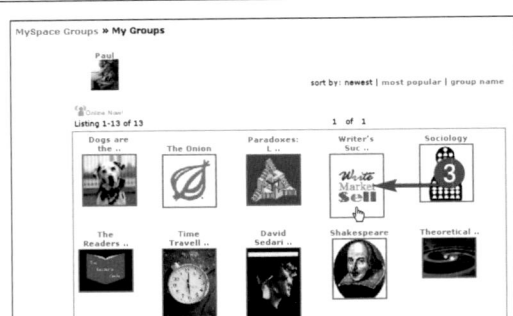

MySpace displays the group's profile.

④ Click Resign.

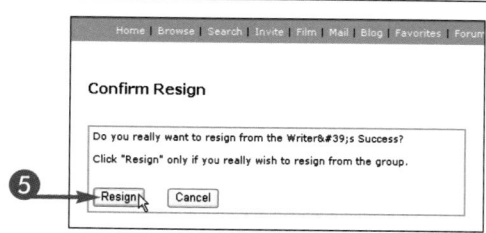

The Confirm Resign page appears.

⑤ Click Resign.

MySpace resigns you from the group.

Try This!

Rather than resigning from a group, you may enjoy a group so much that you want other people to share it with you. To invite a person to join the group, navigate to the person's profile page and then click the Add to Group link in his Contacting tab. In the list of your groups that MySpace displays, click the group you want the person to join, and then click Add to Group. This sends an e-mail to the person, and he or she then clicks either Approve or Deny.

87

How a little over

Create Your Own Group

If no MySpace group is right for you, you can create and moderate your own group.

Despite the huge number of groups that MySpace offers, you may not find a group that suits your needs. You may have a new or obscure topic that no one else has thought of, or you may prefer a discussion board just for certain friends, colleagues, or family members. For these and similar situations, you can create your own group. MySpace sets you up as the group moderator and gives you a great deal of control over how the group operates and who can join it.

Note that you need to have had a MySpace account for at least seven days before you can create a group.

---

① Click Groups.

② Click Create Group.

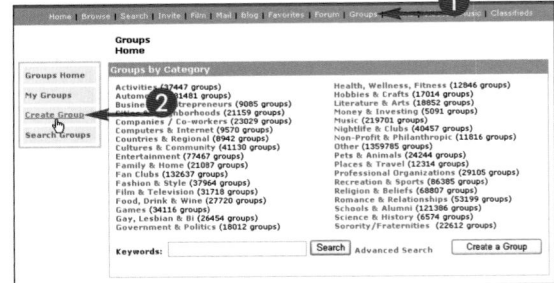

The Create a Group on MySpace page appears.

③ Type a Group Name.

④ Click a Category.

⑤ Click the group options you prefer (○ changes to ⊙).

⑥ Fill in your location.

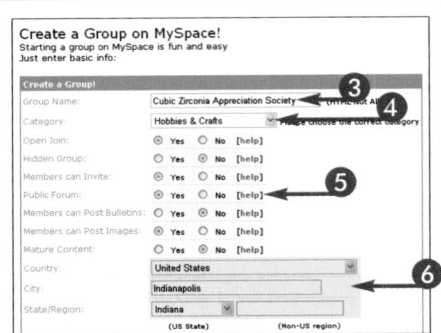

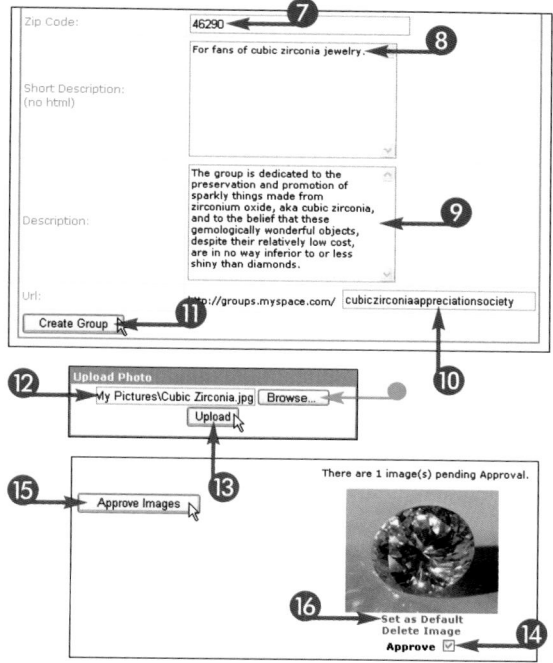

⑦ Type your Zip Code.

⑧ Type a Short Description of the group.

⑨ Type a longer Description of the group.

Note: You can format your longer Description with HTML tags.

⑩ Type the URL you want to use for the group.

⑪ Click Create Group.

The Upload Some Photos page appears.

⑫ Type the location of a photo on your computer.

● You can also click Browse, click the photo in the Choose File dialog box, and click Open.

⑬ Click Upload.

MySpace asks you to approve the image.

⑭ Click Approve (☐ changes to ☑).

⑮ Click Approve Images.

⑯ Click Set as Default.

MySpace creates the group.

More Options!
After you create your group, MySpace adds it to the My Groups page, where it appears with "Moderator" below the group icon. To make changes to the groups, click Groups, click My Groups, and then click the group icon. In the group's profile page, click Edit Group to make changes to the group's configuration.

If you have an item or service to sell or if you are looking for a job, relationship, or musician for your band, you can post a classified ad on MySpace. Note that you need to have had a MySpace account for at least 7 days before you can post a classified ad.

① Click Classifieds.

● If the city is incorrect, click Change City and then click the city you want to use.

② Click Post Ad.

③ Use this list to click a category.

MySpace adds new controls, which vary depending on the category you choose.

④ Use this list to click a subcategory.

⑤ Fill in the other category details.

⑥ Type a Subject.

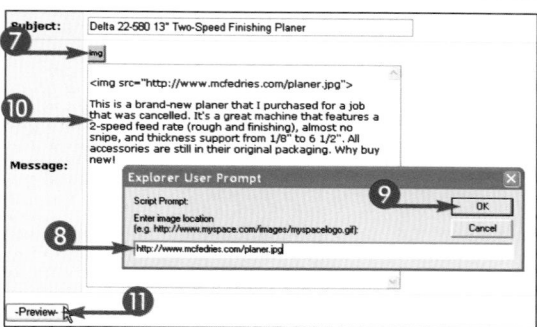

7 To display an image, click Img.

8 Type the Web location of the image.

9 Click OK.

10 Type your ad text.

11 Click Preview.

12 Click Post.

MySpace posts your ad.

Remove It!
To delete a classified ad, click Classifieds, click My Ads, and then click the link for the ad you want to delete. Click Delete and then click OK when MySpace asks you to confirm.

Blogging with MySpace

MySpace includes built-in tools for reading and creating blogs, which are online journals that people use to record their thoughts and ideas, point out interesting links on the Web, or pass along news or information.

For reading blogs, MySpace makes the latest posts available on each member's profile page, but you can also subscribe to a blog to receive notifications of new posts.

For creating blogs, MySpace enables you to compose and format messages online. If you know HTML, you can augment your posts with text formatting, images, and links. MySpace also gives you powerful tools for customizing the look of your blog. With these tools, you can change the colors and fonts, create a custom header, and much more.

Quick Tips

Subscribe to a Blog

You can subscribe to your favorite MySpace blogs, which gives you easy access to those blogs and enables you to receive notifications for new posts.

Keeping up with a MySpace member's blog is straightforward: You navigate to the person's profile page and look at the Latest Blog Entry module, which shows the subject lines of the last five posts. You can then click View More to read a post or click View All Blog Entries.

That works well for a blog or two, but if you read many blogs, it can be time consuming, and you might miss posts. A better approach is to subscribe to your favorite blogs. MySpace maintains a subscription list for you, so you can easily navigate to each blog, and MySpace also sends you e-mail notifications for new blog posts.

---

① Navigate to the profile of the MySpace member to whose blog you want to subscribe.

② Click Subscribe to This Blog.

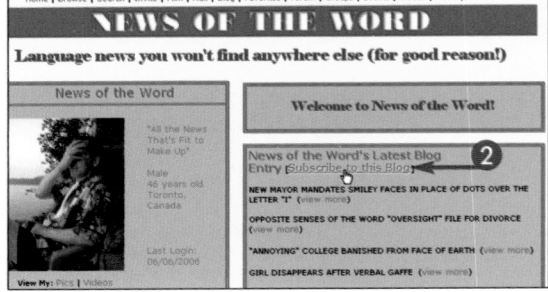

The Confirm Subscribe to Blog page appears.

③ Click Subscribe.

4 You are now subscribed.

Return to Blog Home

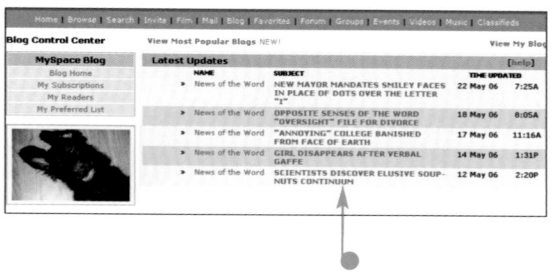

MySpace subscribes you to the blog.

4 Click Return to Blog Home.

Your Blog Control Center page appears.

● The latest posts from your subscribed blog appear here.

Try This!

If you do not know of any good MySpace blogs to read, click View Most Popular Blogs in the Blog Control Center. Alternatively, click Search in the navigation bar, click Blogs in the Search list, and then search for a topic that interests you.

Turn Off Blog Post Notifications

If you are subscribed to many blogs or to a few busy blogs, you can configure MySpace to stop sending you e-mail notifications of new blog posts.

When you subscribe to a blog, MySpace automatically sends you an e-mail message each time a new entry is posted to that blog. This is very handy because it ensures that you do not miss any posts.

On the downside, if you subscribe to many blogs, or if one of your bloggers is particularly prolific, your e-mail Inbox could become overrun with post notifications. If that happens, you can configure some or all of your subscriptions to stop sending out post notifications.

---

① Click Blog.

Your Blog Control Center page appears.

② Click My Subscriptions.

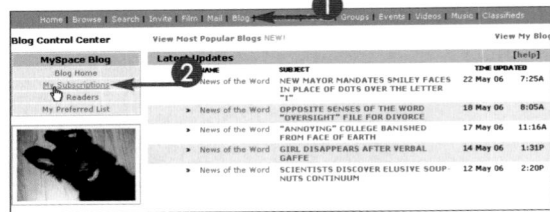

③ Click Edit for the subscription with which you want to work.

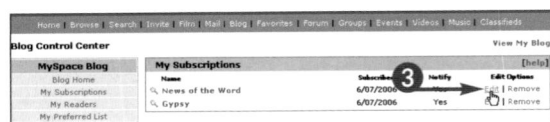

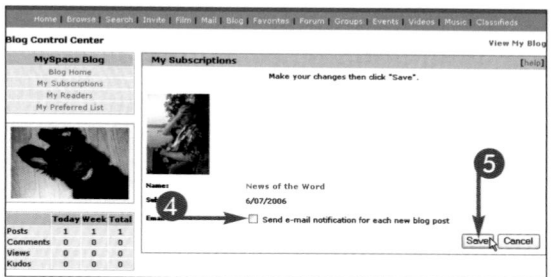

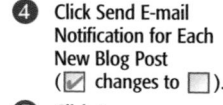

④ Click Send E-mail
Notification for Each
New Blog Post
(☑ changes to ☐).

⑤ Click Save.

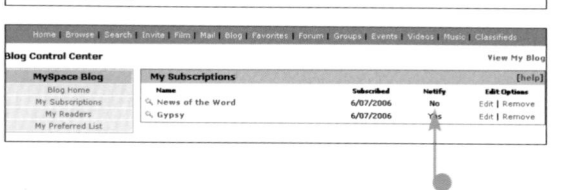

MySpace configures the
subscription to not send
notifications.

● The subscription shows
No in the Notify column.

Try This!

You can also keep up to date on a blog's posts by using Real Simple
Syndication (RSS). This is a technology that maintains a list of recent
posts in XML format. Using an RSS reader program, you can add
the blog's RSS feed and view the latest posts in the reader. To get a
MySpace blog's RSS feed address, view the blog, right-click the RSS
link, and then click Copy Shortcut.

Unsubscribe from a Blog

If you do not have time to read a blog, or if you are subscribed to a blog that is no longer interesting, you can unsubscribe from that blog.

One of the unwritten rules of blogging is that bloggers must post new entries regularly. This means that most serious bloggers post entries at least several times a week, and some even post several times a day. It takes time to read all those posts, so you may find that you do not have enough time in the day to keep up. Alternatively, not all blogs are very good, so you may find that a blog you have subscribed to is not worth reading. In both cases, you can unsubscribe from a blog to remove it from your subscription list.

---

① Click Blog.

Your Blog Control Center page appears.

② Click My Subscriptions.

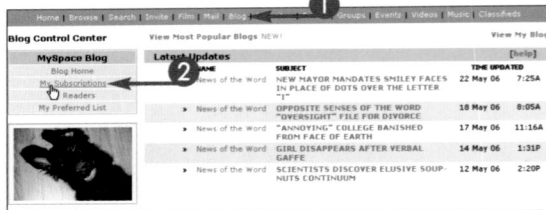

③ Click Remove for the subscription you want to stop.

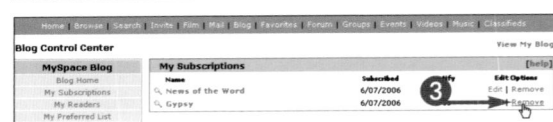

MySpace asks you to confirm.

 Click OK.

MySpace removes the blog from your subscription list.

More Options!

You can also unsubscribe from a blog directly, which is handy if you are currently reading a subscribed blog and realize that you do not want to keep your subscription. Look for the Unsubscribe link at the top of a blog post or below the member's picture. Note that MySpace does *not* ask you to confirm, so be sure you want to unsubscribe before continuing. If you are sure, click the Unsubscribe link.

You can become a MySpace blogger by posting entries to your own blog.

Every MySpace member has his or her own blog (MySpace sometimes calls it a journal, but no one else does). One of the great things about MySpace is that you do not need to do anything to set up your blog. MySpace has already done all the hard work for you, so you just need to think of something to say and then post it. However, most blogs do have a particular theme, so you should give some thought about what your own theme will be before you start posting.

① Click Home.

② Click Blog.

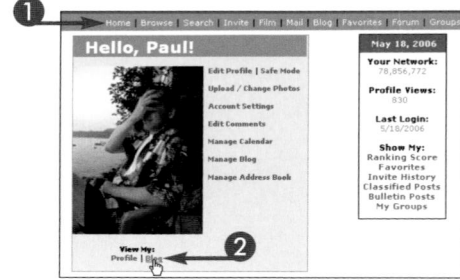

Your blog page appears.

③ Click Post New Blog.

Note: *You can also click Blog in the navigation bar and then click Post New Blog.*

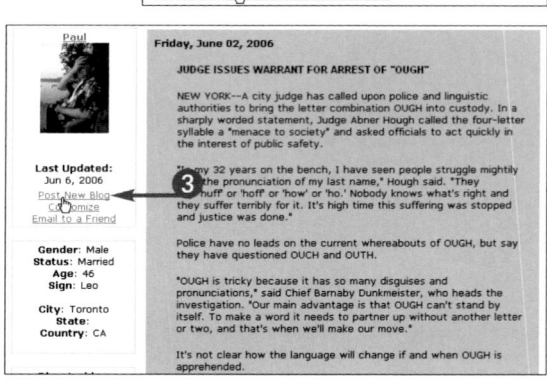

The Post a New Blog Entry page appears.

4 Specify the Posted Date.

5 Specify the Posted Time.

6 Type the Subject of the post.

7 Use the Category list to click the category of the post.

8 Type the post Body.

● Use these controls to format the selected text.

9 Click Preview & Post.

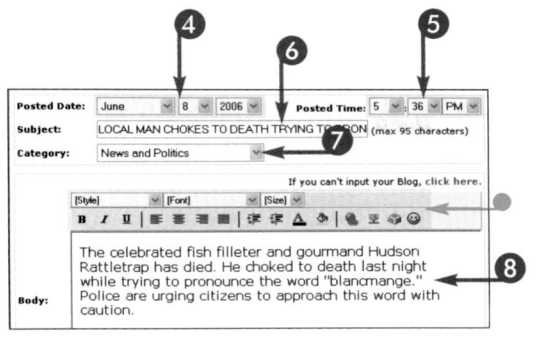

My Space displays a preview of the post.

10 Click Post Blog.

MySpace posts the blog entry.

More Options!

If you know HTML and CSS, you can use that knowledge to control the look and layout of your blog post. In the Post a New Blog Entry page, click View Source (☐ changes to ☑). This hides the formatting controls and shows you the source code underlying the post body. Add your own HTML and inline CSS code. See Chapters 2 and 3 for more about HTML and CSS.

Customize
Your Blog Page

You can improve the look of your blog by customizing page components such as the background color, font, and link colors.

Chapters 2 and 3 explained that customizing your MySpace profile requires extensive and often complex tweaking with CSS codes and HTML tags. Fortunately, this does not apply to your blog. Although it is possible to use CSS and HTML to customize the look of your blog, MySpace offers a lot of customization options. For the general page settings, MySpace enables you to set the background color, the alignment of the posts on the page, the width of the blog, the default font family, font size, and font color, the color of your links, and the number of posts that appear on each page.

---

① Click Home.

② Click Blog.

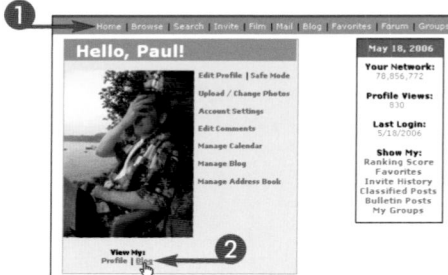

Your blog page appears.

③ Click Customize.

Note: You can also click Blog in the navigation bar and then click Customize Blog.

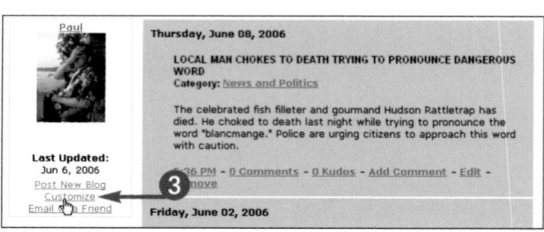

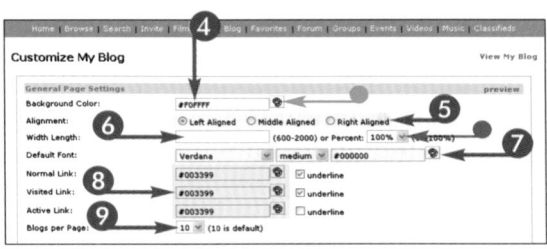

The Customize My Blog page appears.

④ Type the code for the Background Color.

● For all color fields, you can click the Palette icon to display a palette of clickable colors.

⑤ Click how you want the blog aligned on the page (○ changes to ⊙).

⑥ Type the blog width, in pixels.

● You can also set the width as a percentage of the browser window width.

⑦ Use these options to choose the default font family, size, and color.

⑧ Use these text boxes to type color codes for the normal, visited, and active links.

⑨ Click the number of posts you want to appear on each page.

⑩ Scroll to the bottom of the page and click Update.

MySpace updates your blog page settings.

Important!
Note that MySpace offers a huge range of blog customization options, and this task just covers a few of them. See the next four tasks to learn more ways to customize your blog.

Create a Custom Blog Header

You can give your blog a unique identity by crafting a custom blog header. When readers view your blog, the only identification they see is your profile name and picture in the sidebar to the left of the posts. Successful blogs have good content, of course, but they also have strong identities that make them unique and immediately recognizable. You are on your own as far as the content goes, but

MySpace can help with the identity part. The Customize My Blog page includes a Page Header section that enables you to define both a site name and a tagline that appear in a table above your blog. You can customize the font family, size, and color for both the name and tagline, as well as specify the table's border and interior colors.

① Click Home.

② Click Blog.

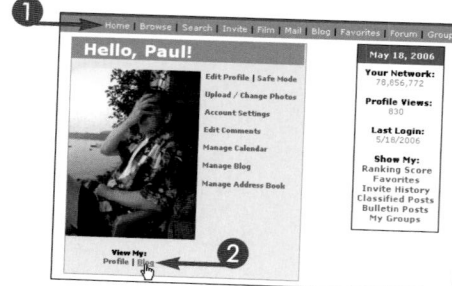

Your blog page appears.

③ Click Customize.

Note: You can also click Blog in the navigation bar and then click Customize Blog.

The Customize My Blog page appears.

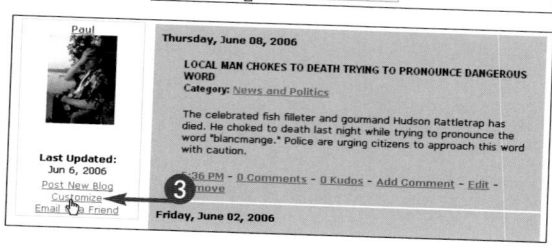

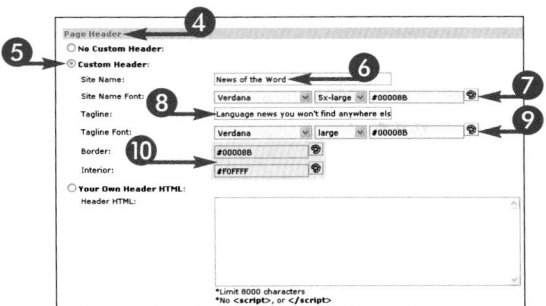

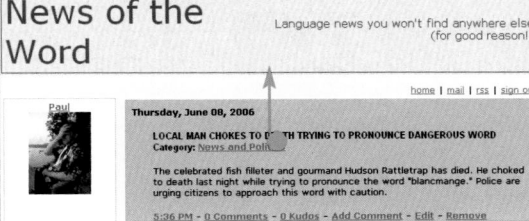

④ Scroll down to the Page Header section.

⑤ Click Custom Header (○ changes to ◉).

⑥ Type your Site Name.

⑦ Use these controls to set the site name font family, size, and color.

⑧ Type your blog Tagline.

⑨ Use these controls to set the tagline font family, size, and color.

⑩ Type the color codes for the Border and Interior.

⑪ Scroll to the bottom of the page and click Update.

● MySpace updates your blog page with your custom header.

TIP

More Options!
The Page Header section also enables you to define your header using your own HTML tags. Click Your Own Header HTML (○ changes to ◉), and then type your HTML tags in the Header HTML text box. For example, if you have an image on another Web site that you want to use as the header, insert the `<img>` tag in the Header HTML box:

`<img src="url">`

Replace *url* with the address of the image.

Customize the Side Module Layout

You can customize the blog page's side module to integrate it with the rest of the blog as well as control the personal information it displays.

The table that appears to the left of the blog posts is called the *side module*. The top section displays your profile name and picture, your online status, and some links, and the bottom section enables readers to navigate your archives. The middle section shows personal data, including your gender, marital status, age, and city.

The Customize My Blog page includes a Side Module section that enables you to customize the middle section, including what information is displayed and how the text is aligned. You can also customize the position of the entire side module (left or right) as well as the colors of its font, border, and interior.

---

① Click Home.

② Click Blog.

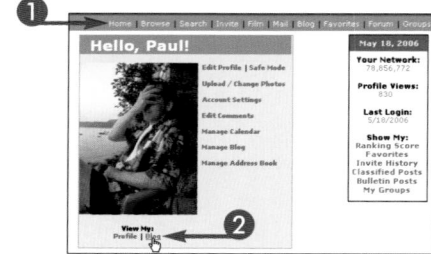

Your blog page appears.

③ Click Customize.

Note: *You can also click Blog in the navigation bar and then click Customize Blog.*

The Customize My Blog page appears.

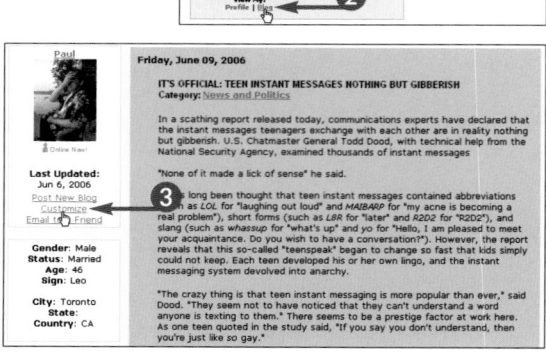

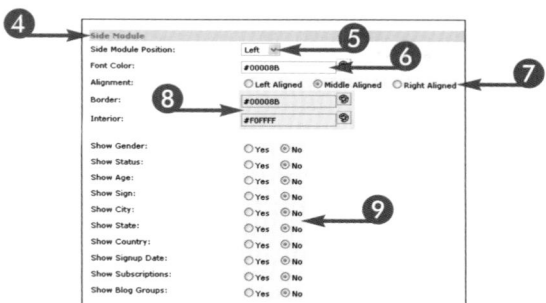

④ Scroll down to the Side Module section.

⑤ Use the Side Module Position list to click the position of the module.

⑥ Type a code for the Font Color.

⑦ Click the Alignment of the middle section (○ changes to ⊙).

⑧ Type the color codes for the Border and Interior.

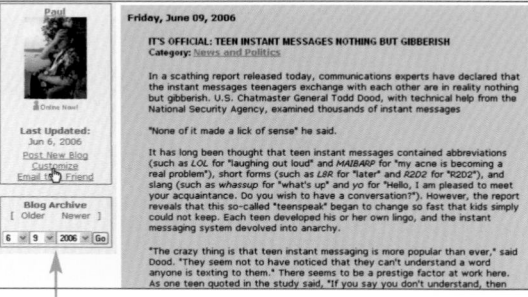

⑨ Click Yes to display personal data, or No to hide it (○ changes to ⊙).

⑩ Scroll to the bottom of the page and click Update.

● MySpace updates your blog page side module.

TIP

Did You Know?

If you prefer to let your blog posts speak for themselves, you can disable the middle section of the side module that displays your personal information. In the Side Module section of the Customize My Blog page, click No for each of the Show options (○ changes to ⊙), and then click Update. When you view your blog, you will see that MySpace does not display the middle section of the side module.

Customize Your Blog Posts and Comments

You can customize the font, background, and layout of your blog posts and comments to personalize your blog and to coordinate your posts and comments with the rest of the blog page.

The blog posts are the heart of your blog, so you want them to have a unique, readable look that fits in with the rest of the page. The Customize My Blog page includes a Blog Post Settings section that

enables you to customize your posts. You can set the colors of the post and date backgrounds and the spacer that separates posts. You can also set the date format and alignment, the font of the subject text, the time format and position, and the post indent. There is also a Comment Post Settings section that you can use to format various comment colors.

---

① Click Home.

② Click Blog.

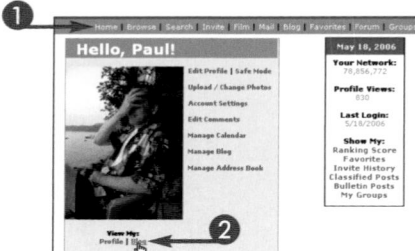

Your blog page appears.

③ Click Customize.

Note: *You can also click Blog in the navigation bar and then click Customize Blog.*

The Customize My Blog page appears.

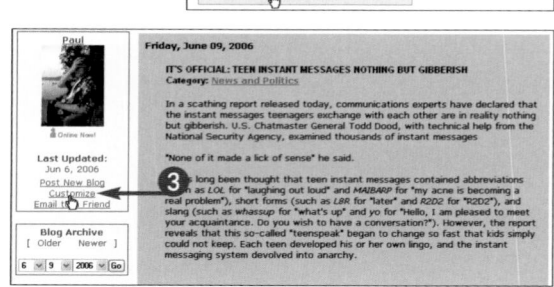

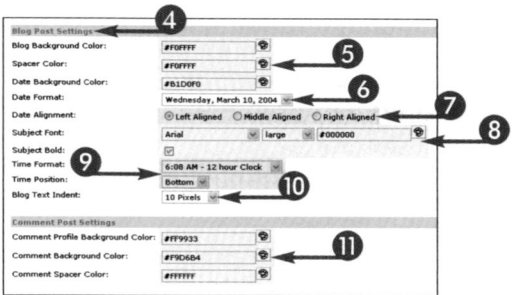

④ Scroll down to the Blog Post Settings section.

⑤ Type a code for the Blog Background, Spacer, and Date Background colors.

⑥ Use the Date Format list to click a date format.

⑦ Click a Date Alignment option (○ changes to ●).

⑧ Use these controls to set the Subject Font.

⑨ Use these lists to click a time format and position.

⑩ Use the Blog Text Indent list to click the number of pixels you want the blog posts indented from the left.

⑪ Type a code for the Comment Profile Background, Comment Background, and Comment Spacer colors.

⑫ Scroll to the bottom of the page and click Update.

MySpace updates your blog page posts and comments.

TIP

More Options!

The Customize My Blog page also includes a Background Settings section. Use the Background Image text box to type the address of an image to use as the page background. You can also click Fixed or Scroll (○ changes to ●) and use the Repeat Background list to click whether and how you want the background to repeat to fill the page. You can also use the Music URL text box to specify a music file to play in the background.

Enhance Your Blog with a Custom Style Sheet

You can customize many aspects of your blog page by inserting a custom style sheet that applies styles to the blog page elements.

The Customize My Blog page gives you dozens of options for controlling the look and feel of your blog page. However, you can get an even greater level of control by creating a custom style sheet and applying

styles to the following classes:

Date: `p.blogTimeStamp`

Subject: `p.blogSubject`

Post: `table.blog`

Time (text): `p.blogContentInfo`

Time (links): `p.blogContentInfo a`

Spacer: `tr.spacer`

---

① Click Home.

② Click Blog.

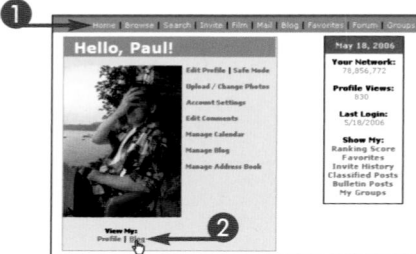

Your blog page appears.

③ Click Customize.

Note: You can also click Blog in the navigation bar and then click Customize Blog.

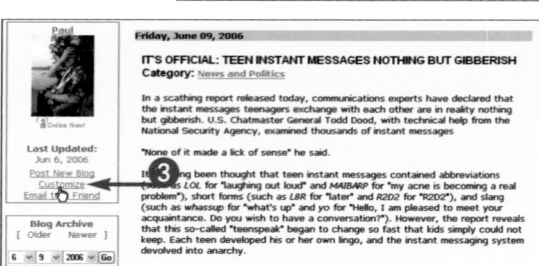

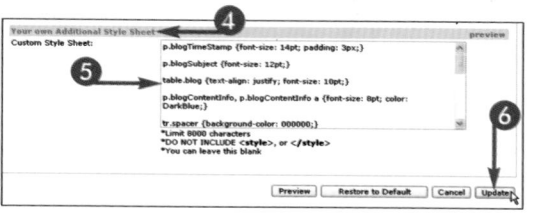

The Customize My Blog page appears.

④ Scroll down to the Your Own Additional Style Sheet section.

⑤ Type the CSS code for the classes you want to customize.

⑥ Click Update.

MySpace updates your blog page posts and comments.

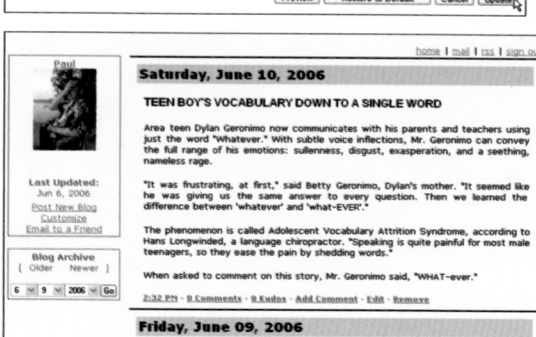

More Options!

MySpace also defines several classes that you can use to customize your comments using CSS:

Background: td.blogCommentsProfile

Comment background: td.blogComments

Comments: p.blogCOmmentsContent

Spacer: tr.commentSpacer

Add a Podcast to a Blog Post

You can augment your blog posts with audio versions called *podcasts* to which other people can subscribe.

Many bloggers create audio versions of their posts and make the resulting MP3 files available via special feeds that people can subscribe to. Because these feeds were originally created for downloading to iPod MP3 players, the audio files are usually called *podcasts*.

MySpace supports podcasts via its RSS feed. You have to do three things: record the audio, put your podcast on the Web, and then add the file's address to your post. The rest is handled automatically by MySpace, and other people can subscribe to your podcasts by plugging the address of your blog's RSS feed into iTunes or whatever program they use to listen to podcasts.

① Click Home.

② Click Blog.

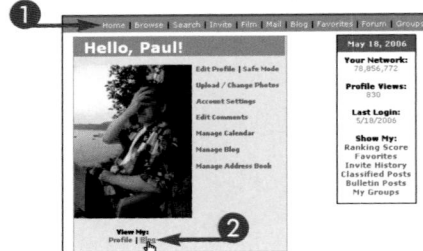

Your blog page appears.

③ Scroll down the blog post to which you want to add the podcast.

④ Click Edit.

● If you want to add a podcast to a new post, click Post New Blog instead.

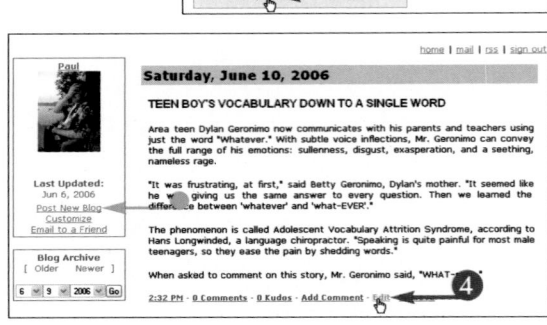

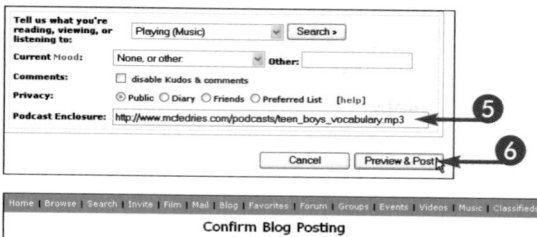

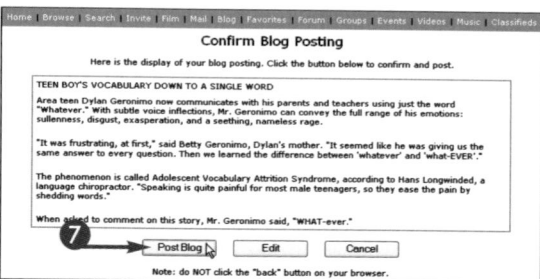

The Edit a Blog Entry page appears.

⑤ Use the Podcast Enclosure text box to type the address of the podcast file.

⑥ Click Preview & Post.

The Confirm Blog Posting page appears.

⑦ Click Post Blog.

MySpace posts the blog entry.

Apply It!

To subscribe to your podcasts, you must first get the address of your RSS feed. Click Home, click Blog, right-click the RSS link, and then click Copy Shortcut. You then paste the RSS address into your podcast software. In iTunes, for example, click Advanced and then click Subscribe to Podcast. In the Subscribe to Podcast dialog box, paste the address of your blog's RSS feed in the URL text box, and then click OK.

Join a Blog Group

You can make it easier for other people to find your blog by setting up your blog within a group of similar blogs.

MySpace maintains several dozen blogging categories, such as Architecture, Pets, Music, and Sports. Within each category you will find a number of *blog groups*, which are blogs that have a similar theme or topic. If you find a group where your blog would fit in, you can join it. This will make it easier for other people to find your blog. MySpace also maintains a link to the blog group in the Blog Control center, so you can easily navigate to the other blogs in your group to catch up on the latest posts.

① **Click Blog.**

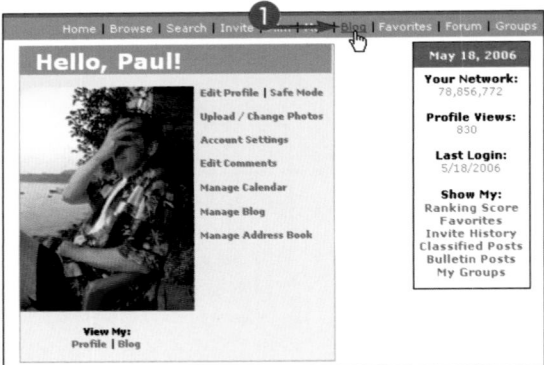

Your Blog Control Center page appears.

② **Click Browse Blog Groups.**

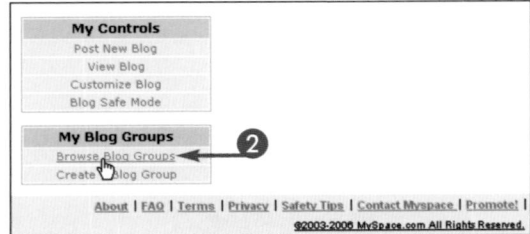

MySpace displays the Browse Blog Groups list.

③ Click the category that contains the group you want to join.

MySpace displays a list of the blog groups in the category.

④ Click the group you want to join.

MySpace displays the group information.

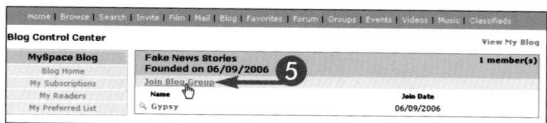

⑤ Click Join Blog Group.

You join the MySpace blog group.

Note: *The group leader may have to approve your blog before you become part of the group.*

Try This!

If you do not see a suitable group, you can create your own group. Click Blog and then click Create a Blog Group. In the Create Blog Group page, type the Blog Group Name, type a Description, and then use the Category list to click the category in which you want your group to appear. If you would like to approve people who want to join your group, click Yes (◯ changes to ◉). Click Create.

Chapter 6

MySpace and Media

MySpace features a variety of multimedia elements you can use to make your profile page more interesting. For example, you can upload songs and videos to play on your profile page, or share your favorite video clips with other users. If you have a favorite band on MySpace, you can add one of their songs to your profile page so it plays automatically whenever another user views your page. This chapter shows you how easy it is to add songs and videos to your MySpace profile.

MySpace is also a popular place for promoting your band or filmmaking work. You can create a special profile page for your band, for example, and add detailed information about your musical influences, likes, and dislikes, and promote your band's Web site. If you are a burgeoning filmmaker, you can do the same to promote your films. This chapter shows you how to create band and filmmaker profile pages and upload your art for others to hear and see.

Quick Tips

Upload a Video to Share

You can upload a video onto MySpace to share with others. For example, you might upload a video clip from a recent birthday party, concert, or sporting event. Public video clips are available for all MySpace users to see. You can also upload a video and keep it private.

The MySpace video form consists of three separate steps you must follow to upload a video clip. Use Step 1 to create a title and description for your video. Step 2 lets you assign a category and keywords, called tags, to the video. Your video may fit into one or several categories, ranging from animals to sports. Use Step 3 to navigate to the file on your computer and upload it to MySpace.

---

① In MySpace, click Videos.

● The Videos home page appears.

② Click Upload.

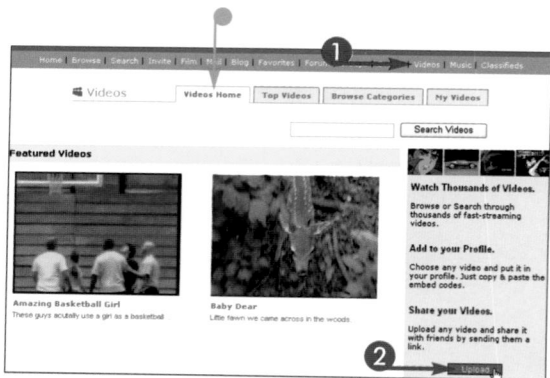

The Upload Video: Step 1 page appears.

③ Type a title for the video.

④ Type a description of the video clip.

⑤ Click whether you want the video to appear as a public or private video (○ changes to ⦿).

⑥ Click the agreement check box (☐ changes to ☑).

⑦ Click Next.

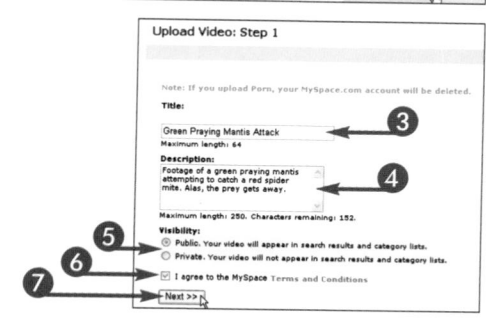

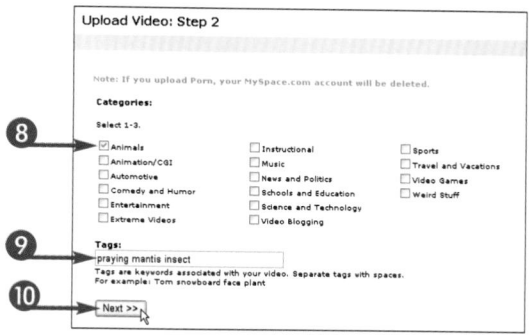

Upload Video: Step 2

Note: If you upload Porn, your MySpace.com account will be deleted.

Categories:

Select 1-3.

☑ Animals	☐ Instructional	☐ Sports
☐ Animation/CGI	☐ Music	☐ Travel and Vacations
☐ Automotive	☐ News and Politics	☐ Video Games
☐ Comedy and Humor	☐ Schools and Education	☐ Weird Stuff
☐ Entertainment	☐ Science and Technology	
☐ Extreme Videos	☐ Video Blogging	

Tags:

praying mantis insect

Tags are keywords associated with your video. Separate tags with spaces.
For example: Tom snowboard face plant

[Next >>]

The Upload Video: Step 2 page appears.

8 Click a category for the video (☐ changes to ☑).

You can assign up to three categories, if needed.

9 Type any tags, or keywords, you want to associate with the video.

Note: *Tags are used with searching MySpace for specific types of video clips.*

10 Click Next.

The Upload Video: Step 3 page appears.

11 Click Browse.

12 Navigate to the video file and double-click the filename.

● MySpace adds the path to the file in the Upload Film section.

13 Click Upload.

MySpace uploads the video clip.

Note: *Depending on the size of the clip and your connection speed, the upload may take a few minutes.*

Did You Know?

The Upload Video form lists all the acceptable file formats. MySpace allows video files as large as 100MB. If you try to upload anything larger, MySpace displays an error message indicating that the file is too large. You can upload a variety of video file formats onto MySpace, including ASF, MOV, QT, MPG, FLV, WMV, 3G2, 3GP, MP4, CMP, DIVX, and more.

You can upload a video onto your MySpace profile so it is readily viewable by anyone reading your profile page. For example, you might upload a video clip from a school event or a sporting activity.

You can use the regular Upload Video form to upload a video to MySpace. After you upload the video, you can copy and paste the video code to your profile's

Interests & Personality section. This places the video clip directly onto your profile page. For example, you can place the video clip in the About Me or Interests category of your profile. When you save your profile changes, the embedded video code is added to your profile's HTML coding. Anyone viewing your profile page can play the video clip.

① Upload a video clip to MySpace.

Note: *See the previous task, "Upload a Video to Share," to learn how to upload a video.*

② Click Videos.

③ Click My Videos.

MySpace displays your video clips.

④ Click View for the video you want to add.

The video window appears.

⑤ Double-click the Video Code text box.

⑥ Press Ctrl+C.

The coding is copied to the Clipboard.

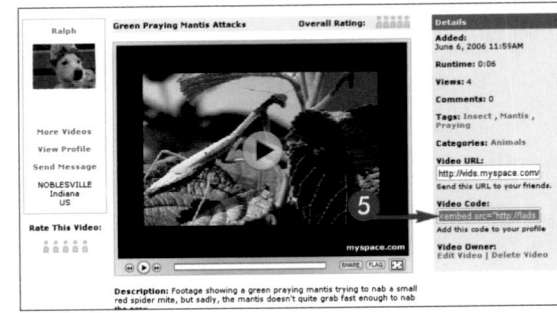

7 Click Home.

8 Click Edit Profile.

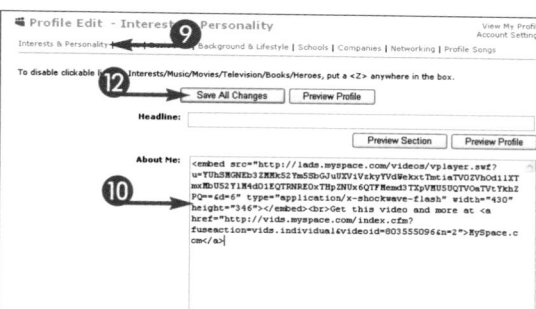

The Profile Edit - Interests & Personality page appears.

9 Click Interests & Personality.

10 Click in the text box where you want to insert the video clip.

11 Press Ctrl+V.

The video code is added to your profile.

12 Click Save All Changes.

You can now view the video clip on your profile page.

Delete It!

You can easily remove video clips you add to your MySpace account. Simply open the Videos page, click the My Videos tab, and then click the Delete link for the video you want to remove. To remove a video clip associated with your profile page, edit your profile and delete the video coding.

You can add a MySpace song to your profile. When you run across a song you like on MySpace, such as a song from a featured or favorite band, you can assign it to your profile. When you add a song, it plays automatically whenever other users view your profile.

Profile songs appear in their own little player boxes located on the profile page. When a song ends, users can click the Play button again to replay the song. Users can also click the player box to link to the associated Web page displaying more details about the artist.

① From MySpace, click Music.

The MySpace Music page appears.

② Browse through the genres or artists to locate a song you want to add.

● You can click a song to play it.

● You can use the player controls to pause or stop a song.

③ When you find a song you like, click Add.

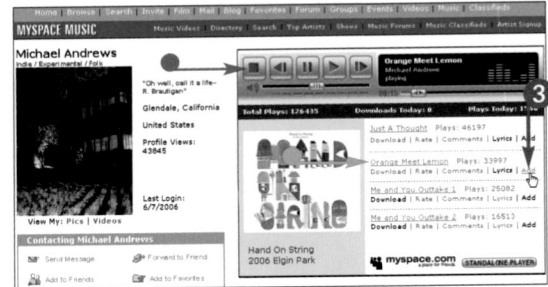

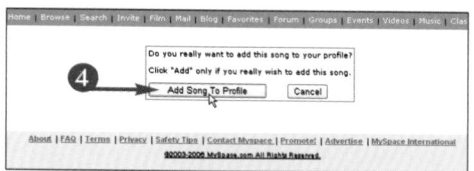

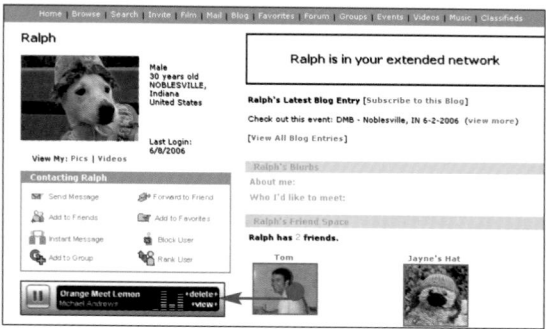

MySpace asks you to confirm the addition.

④ Click Add Song To Profile.

The song is added to your profile.

You can view your profile at any time and hear the song.

● The song appears as a player box on the profile page.

Delete It!

To remove a song from your profile, first display your profile page, and then click the Delete option on the player box. MySpace opens the Delete Profile Song form. Click Delete and MySpace removes the song from your profile page.

Create a Band Profile

If you have a band or musical group of any kind, you can create a unique profile page on MySpace to promote your music. When you create a band profile, MySpace allows you to upload four MP3 files showcasing your original songs, plus you can create a URL especially for your group and send the link to others to view.

Band profiles work a bit differently than regular MySpace profiles. For example, you can post information about upcoming concerts to appear as listed dates on your band's profile page, create member bios, add information about musical influences and record labels, and more.

① From MySpace, click Music.

The MySpace Music page displays.

② Click Artist Signup.

The Sign Up page appears.

③ Complete the fields to fill out the information, including your band name, e-mail, and genre.

④ Click the Terms of Service check box (☐ changes to ☑).

⑤ Click Sign Up.

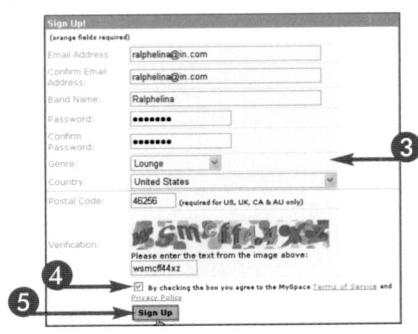

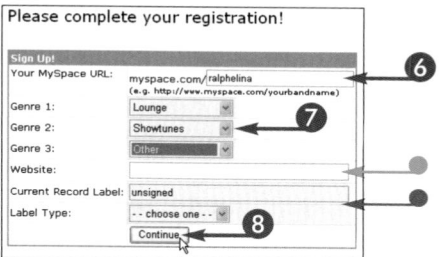

MySpace asks you to complete the registration.

6 Fill in the MySpace URL with your band name.

7 Use the Genre drop-down lists to select a musical type for your group.

● If you have a Web site, add the URL here.

● You can enter any record label information here.

8 Click Continue.

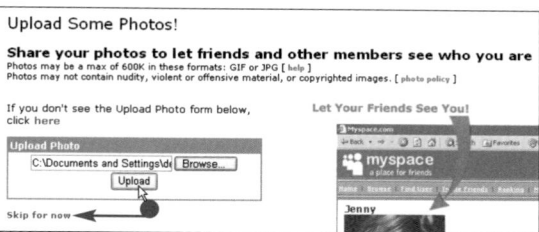

You can continue adding photos or songs to your profile by following the MySpace prompts. For example, the next window asks if you want to upload a photo of your band.

● Click here to skip the remainder of the signup process.

Note: *You can return to your profile page and edit the information, photos, and songs. See the next task, "Edit a Band Profile," to learn more.*

MySpace creates your band profile.

Did You Know?

You can also convert an existing profile into a band profile. To do so, simply log on to your MySpace account and type the following URL into your browser's address bar:

http://collect.myspace.com/index.cfm?fuseaction=BandProfile.convert

Note that once you convert a profile, you cannot return it to a regular profile again.

Edit a Band Profile

If you create a band profile, you can edit the profile to include pertinent information about your band. For example, you can type a detailed bio about your band and how it got started. You can include information about each band member, describe your musical influences, and let others know about your record label.

Although the band profile form includes five different parts, you use the Band Details page to enter detailed information about your group. The band profile form lets you add information for each area, such as a headline or a Web site.

① From MySpace, click Home.

② Click Edit Profile.

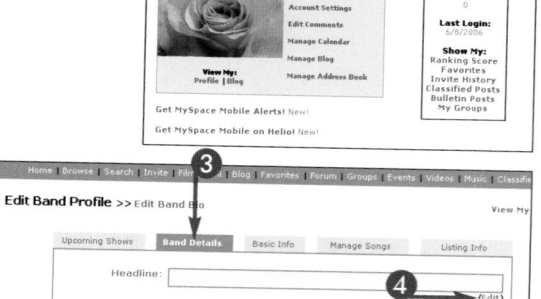

The Edit Band Bio page appears, displaying the Upcoming Shows form by default.

③ Click Band Details.

MySpace displays the Band Details form.

④ Click Edit for the field to which you want to add information.

The Band Details form displays an empty text field for you to edit.

⑤ Type your band information.

⑥ Click Preview.

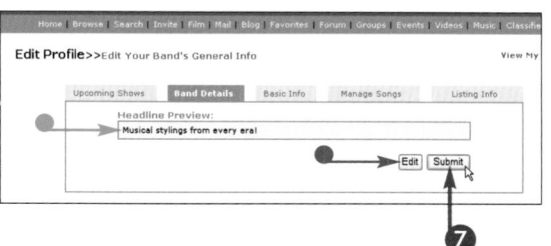

● The Band Details form displays a preview of your entry.

⑦ To keep the changes, click Submit.

● To add further edits to the information, click Edit to return to the previous window and make your changes.

You can continue editing other profile fields as needed.

Note: *You can return to your profile page and edit the information, photos, and songs.*

Did You Know?
The other four parts of the band profile form allow you to enter information about upcoming shows, manage songs you upload to your profile, view listing information, and view the information you used to create the account. Simply click a tab to view the page.

Music is a popular part of MySpace, and if you want to promote your band, you can upload an MP3 song and allow other users to hear your music. You can upload up to four songs to your band profile on MySpace. You must own the copyright to any music you upload to MySpace.

When you upload a song, any users viewing your band profile page can listen to the song. If you select the download option, users can also download the song and listen to it offline as well. If the ranking option is turned on, other users can also rank their opinion of your song on a scale of 1 to 10.

① Open the Edit Profile page to edit your band profile.

Note: See the task "Edit a Band Profile" to learn how to open the Edit Profile form.

② Click Manage Songs.

The Manage Songs page appears.

③ Click Add a Song.

● You can turn these page settings on or off depending on how you want the profile page song to play.

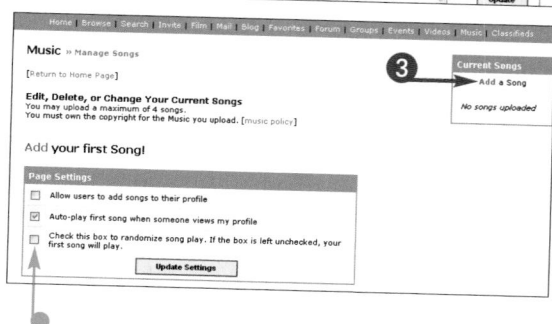

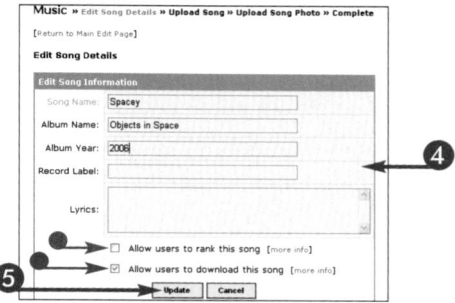

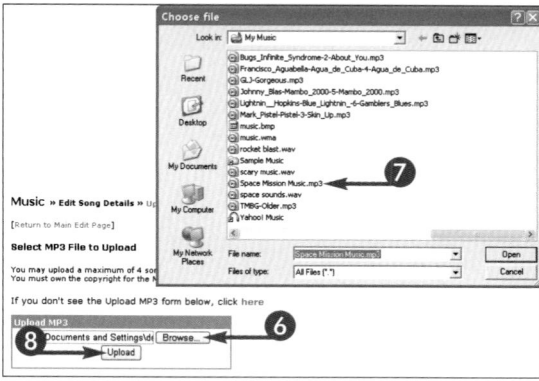

The Edit Song Details form appears.

④ Fill in the song information as needed.

● Click this option to allow users to rank your song (☐ changes to ☑).

● Click this option to let other users download the song (☐ changes to ☑).

⑤ Click Update.

The Select MP3 File to Upload page appears.

⑥ Click Browse.

The Choose File dialog box opens.

⑦ Double-click the song file you want to upload.

⑧ Click Upload.

MySpace uploads the song file to your profile page and prompts you to select a photo to go with the song, if desired.

Note: *You can return to your profile page and edit the information, photos, and songs.*

Delete It!
To remove a song from your profile page, return to the Edit Profile form, click the Manage Songs tab, and then click the Delete button next to the song you want to remove. MySpace immediately removes the song from your profile.

Announce an Upcoming Show for Your Band

Self-promotion is an important part of advertising your presence on MySpace, and if you want to promote your band, you can do so by announcing upcoming shows on your band's profile page. Your profile page lists upcoming shows in the upper right corner of the page. You can list multiple shows as needed.

You can use the Edit Upcoming Shows form, part of the Edit Profile form, to describe upcoming show dates and venues. The form also includes an option for describing the show as well as a place for mentioning any cover costs or ticket prices associated with the show.

① **From MySpace, click Home.**

② **Click Edit Profile.**

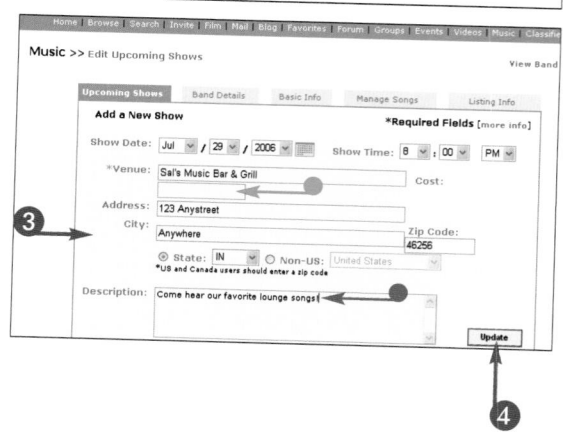

The profile's Edit form appears, displaying the Upcoming Shows information by default.

③ **Fill out the show's details, including date, time, and venue.**

● You can type the cost for the show here.

● You can add a description about the show using this field.

④ **Click Update.**

The Preview Show page appears.

⑤ Check over the information and click Save Show.

● To return to the previous page and make changes, click here.

● MySpace saves the show information and places it on your band's profile page.

Delete It!
To remove a show from the list of upcoming concerts, you can return to the Upcoming Shows page of the Edit Band Profile form and delete the item. Simply scroll to the bottom of the form to see the listed shows, and then click the Delete link next to the show you want to remove.

Create a Filmmaker Profile

If you are an avid filmmaker, you can create your own filmmaker profile on MySpace and share your work with other film aficionados. With a filmmaker profile, you can describe details about your filmmaking process, upload films for others to view, and announce upcoming screenings.

When you create a filmmaker profile, the MySpace form includes a section for entering additional information about your filmmaking roles, status, influences, festival appearances, and professional affiliations. At the end of the account process, you can upload photos to associate with your profile, if desired.

---

① From MySpace, click Film.

The MySpace Film page appears.

② Click Filmmaker Signup.

The signup form page appears.

③ Complete the fields to fill out the information.

④ Click the Terms of Service check box (changes to ☑).

⑤ Click Sign Up.

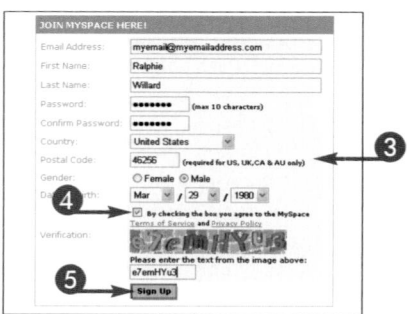

Please complete your registration!

ADDITIONAL INFO

Role 1: Director
Role 2: Screenwriter
Role 3: Cinematographer ⑥
Status: Amateur
Website:
Influences: Film noir
Favorite Directors: Terry Gilliam, George Miller
Awards:
Festivals:
Professional Affiliations:
Continue ⑦

MySpace asks you to complete the registration.

⑥ Use the Role and Status drop-down lists to select the types of filmmaker roles you play.

● If you have a Web site, add the URL here.

● You can enter any additional influences, favorite directors, awards, and professional affiliations here.

⑦ Click Continue.

Home | Browse | Search | Invite | Film | Mail | Blog | Favorites | Forum | Groups | Events | Videos | Music

Upload Some Photos!

Let Your Friends See You!

Share your photos to let your friends and other members see who you are!

Photos may be a max of 600K in these formats: GIF of JPG. [help]

Photos may not contain nudity, violent or offensive material, or copyrighted images. [photo policy]

If you don't see the Upload Photo form below, click here

Upload Photo
[   ] Browse...
Upload

Skip for now

You can continue adding photos to your profile by following the MySpace prompts. For example, the next window asks if you want to upload a photo.

● Click here to skip the remainder of the signup process.

Note: *You can return to your profile page and edit the information, photos, and songs. See the next task to learn more.*

MySpace creates your filmmaker profile.

Did You Know?

You can convert a regular profile to a filmmaker profile using a special code. To do so, simply log on to your MySpace account and type the following URL into your browser's address bar:

http://collect.myspace.com/index.cfm?fuseaction=filmmaker.convert

Note that once you convert a profile, you cannot return it to a regular profile again.

Edit a Filmmaker Profile

If you create a filmmaker profile, you can edit the profile at any time to update information or add information about your work. For example, you can type detailed information about the various roles you take as a filmmaker, what types of films influence your work, what directors you admire, and more. You can include information about your Web site,

and list any awards, festivals, or professional affiliations you might have.

Although the filmmaker profile form includes four different parts, you use the Film Maker Details page to enter detailed information about your filmmaking aspirations.

① **From MySpace, click Home.**

② **Click Edit Profile.**

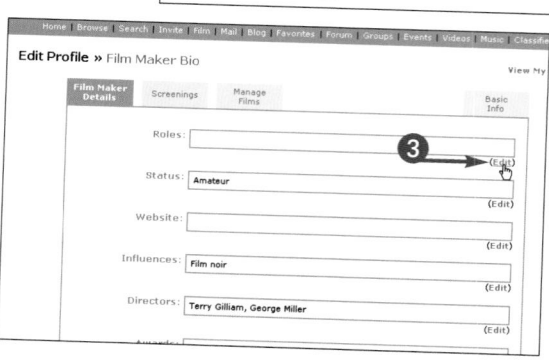

The Film Maker Bio page appears, displaying the Film Maker Details page by default.

③ **Click Edit for the field to which you want to add information.**

The form displays an empty text field for you to edit or drop-down selections you can make.

④ Type your information or choose from the options.

⑤ Click Submit.

● The Film Maker Bio page displays your changes.

You can continue editing other profile fields as needed.

Note: You can return to your profile page and edit the information, photos, and songs.

Did You Know?

The other three parts of the Film Maker Bio page allow you to enter information about upcoming screenings, manage films you upload to MySpace, and view the information you used to create the account. Simply click a tab to view the page.

You can share your filmmaking art with other users on MySpace by uploading your film files. Many burgeoning filmmakers use MySpace to upload trailers for their films. MySpace allows file uploads of up to 100MB. You can upload Windows Media, AVI, MPEG/MPG,

MP4, FLV, RealMedia, and QuickTime file formats. You must own the copyright to any film you upload to MySpace.

When you upload a film, any users viewing your filmmaker profile page can view the film.

---

① From your MySpace home page, open the Edit Profile form.

Note: See the previous task, "Edit a Filmmaker Profile," to learn how to view the Edit Profile form.

MySpace opens the Edit Profile page and displays the Film Maker Bio form by default.

② Click Manage Films.

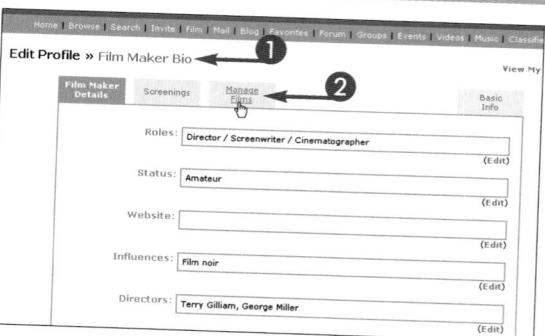

The Manage Films form appears.

③ Fill out the information about the film you want to upload.

④ Click Go to Step 2.

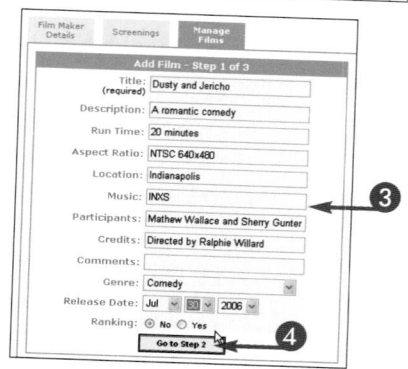

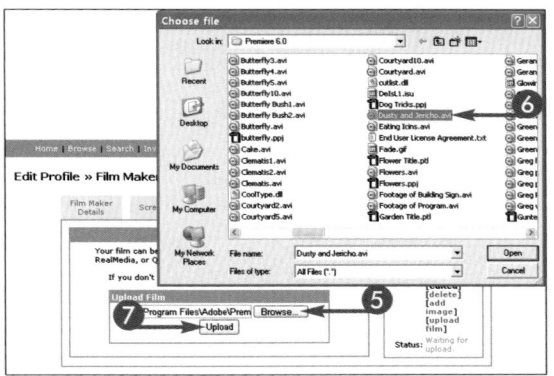

⑤ Click Browse.

The Choose File dialog box opens.

⑥ Double-click the file you want to upload.

⑦ Click Upload.

MySpace uploads the file. Depending on the size of the file, the upload may take a few minutes.

● You can check the status of the film here. MySpace must approve of the film in order to complete the upload process.

Delete It!

To remove a film from your profile page, return to the Edit Profile form, click the Manage Films tab, and then click the Delete button next to the film you want to remove. MySpace immediately removes the film from your profile.

You can advertise your latest filmmaking accomplishments on MySpace by announcing upcoming screenings on your filmmaker profile page. Your profile page lists upcoming screenings in the upper right corner of the page. You can list multiple screenings as needed.

You can use the Film Maker Screenings form, part of the Edit Profile form, to describe upcoming screening dates and

venues. The form also includes an option for describing the screening as well as a place for mentioning any costs or ticket prices associated with the screening.

Once you submit the information, MySpace adds it to your profile page automatically. You can revisit the form page to make changes to the information at any time.

---

① From your MySpace home page, open the Edit Profile form.

Note: See the "Edit a Filmmaker Profile" task to learn how to view the Edit Profile form.

MySpace opens the Edit Profile page and displays the Film Maker Bio form by default.

② Click Screenings.

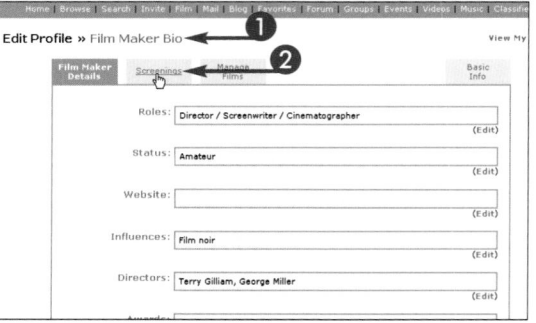

③ Fill out the screening details, including date, time, and venue.

● You can add a description about the show using this field.

④ Click Update.

● MySpace displays a listing about the screening at the bottom of the form.

● To edit the information at any time, click Edit and make your changes.

● MySpace also saves the screening information and places it on your filmmaker profile page.

TIP

Delete It!
To remove a screening from the list of upcoming screenings, you can return to the Film Maker Screenings page of the Edit Profile form and delete the item. Simply scroll to the bottom of the form to see the listed screening, and then click the Delete link next to the screening you want to remove.

Working with MySpace Events

A MySpace event can advertise anything from an upcoming concert, party, film showing, promotional event, or any other type of gathering. You can use events to get the word out about a particular band's scheduled appearance, let others know about a school function, or simply advertise an informal party. You can create your own events in MySpace and invite others to participate, set reminders for other users' events, and add events to your MySpace calendar.

Public events are posted on the MySpace Events page, while private events are only viewable by select users. In addition to listing events, you can also bring more attention to an event through a blog or bulletin. This chapter shows you how to use the MySpace event tools to promote your favorite events online.

Quick Tips

Post a Public Event

You can use MySpace to promote a public event, such as an upcoming concert, conference, school event, or party. Events can include any type of gathering or special promotion, such as a film or television show viewing, a community event, or even a sports party.

When creating an event on MySpace, you can choose to create a public event, such as a band concert, or a private event, such

as a birthday party. A public event is displayed for anyone to view on the Events page, and a private event is only available to the people you invite. You can use the Create An Event form to assign a name for the event, set an event type, and write a description of the event. You can also specify the event start date and time, and the place or venue for the event.

---

① In MySpace, click Events.

② Click Create Event.

● You can also click the Create New Event link.

The Create An Event window appears.

③ Fill out the event form as needed, adding details about the event.

● Type a Name for the event here.

● Click here to assign a Category.

● Enter an event Description here.

Note: *If you create a private event, you can invite select users to the event.*

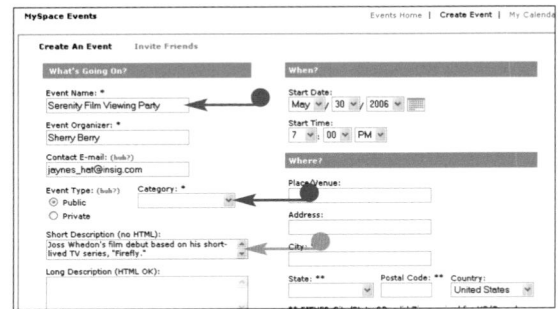

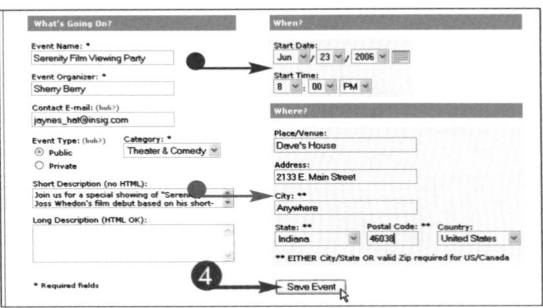

- Select a Start Date and Time for the event using these options.

- Specify the location of the event using these options.

④ Click Save Event.

MySpace saves the event.

- You can view events on the Events home page. You can click the Events link at any time to view the events listings.

- To view details about an event, click the event name.

Note: You can also display your MySpace calendar and view your events as they appear listed on the calendar.

Try It!
You can upload a picture to include with your event information on MySpace. To do so, click the event and click the Upload/Change Image link. This opens the Upload Photo form, and you can designate an image to include with the event. To learn more about uploading pictures onto MySpace, see Chapter 1.

Get Reminded of Your Events

You can use the MySpace calendar feature to remind yourself of upcoming events, such as concerts and parties. You can also use your calendar to make note of upcoming appointments, birthdays, calls you have to make, and more. Once you schedule an item on the calendar, you can send an e-mail reminder about the item to

your MySpace mailbox or to your e-mail address, or both. You can specify the advance time for the reminder, such as a day or a week.

The My Calendar Options form includes options for controlling the display of your calendar as well as reminder options.

---

① In MySpace, click Home.

② Click Manage Calendar.

The Calendar page appears with the current date showing.

③ Click Options.

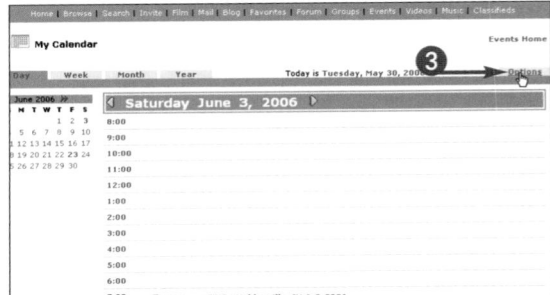

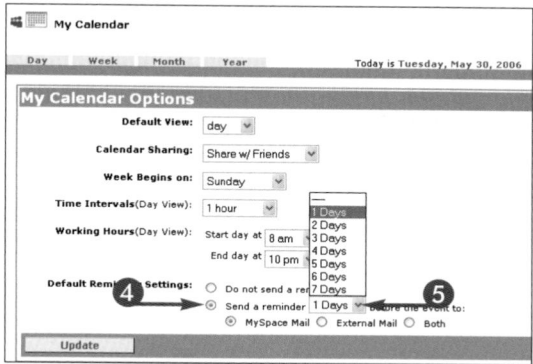

The My Calendar Options form appears.

④ Under the Default Reminder Settings, click Send a Reminder (○ changes to ◉).

⑤ Click here and set how many days in advance you want to be reminded.

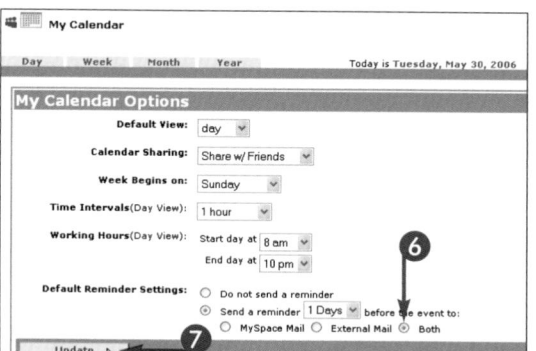

⑥ Click an e-mail option (○ changes to ◉).

⑦ Click Update.

MySpace e-mails you a reminder at the designated advance date.

Try It!

You can use your MySpace calendar to keep track of appointments and other important meetings. For example, if you click the Week or Month view, you can add appointments to the calendar using the Add button. This displays an Add Entry to Calendar form you can fill out with details about the appointment.

Add an Event to Your Calendar

You can use the MySpace calendar feature to keep track of upcoming events you want to attend. MySpace events include everything from concerts, school events, parties, films, and more. MySpace makes it easy to add public events to your personal MySpace calendar. You can add an event directly from any event page. By adding an event to the calendar, you can always view upcoming activities and plan accordingly.

If the MySpace calendar sharing feature is turned on, anyone viewing your profile page can see the events on your calendar. If the friends-only sharing feature is on, only your friends can see your calendar events. If you have the calendar sharing feature turned off, only you can see events listed on your calendar.

ADD AN EVENT TO THE CALENDAR

① Click Events.

② Click the event you want to add to the calendar.

Details about the event appear.

③ Click Add To My Calendar.

The event is immediately added to your personal calendar.

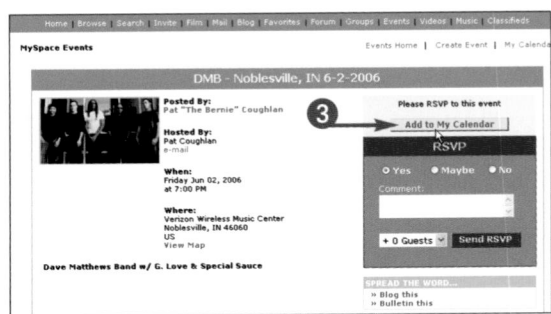

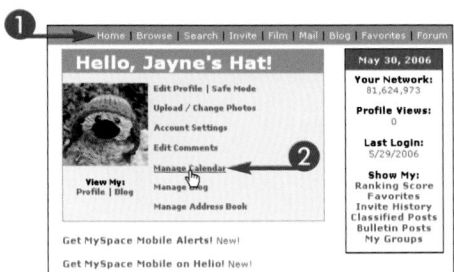

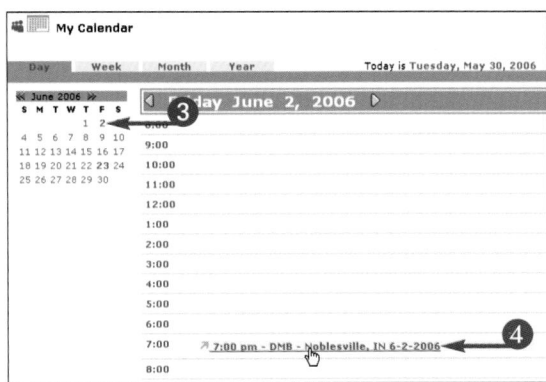

VIEW AN EVENT ON YOUR CALENDAR

① In MySpace, click Home.

② Click Manage Calendar.

You can also click the Calendar link on any Events page to view the calendar.

The My Calendar page appears.

③ Navigate to the date you want to view.

④ Click the event you want to view.

MySpace displays information about the event.

Remove It!

You can remove an event from your calendar just as easily as you added it. To do so, simply click the event name listed in the calendar to open details about the event. Then click the Remove From My Calendar button. MySpace immediately deletes the entry from your calendar.

Blog an Event

You can create a blog for any event in MySpace. For example, you might want to create a blog entry about a particular concert or school function. Your blog entry might include details about the event, your experiences, or a review of the activities. A blog entry might also include information about the event before the event occurs.

When you create an event blog, you can specify whether the blog is viewed by everyone, friends only, or a preferred list of users. After you create your blog, you can review it before posting it online.

---

① Display the event page you want to blog.

Note: *See the "Add an Event to Your Calendar" task to learn how to view event information.*

② Click the Blog This link.

The Post a New Blog Entry form appears.

③ Type in your blog text.

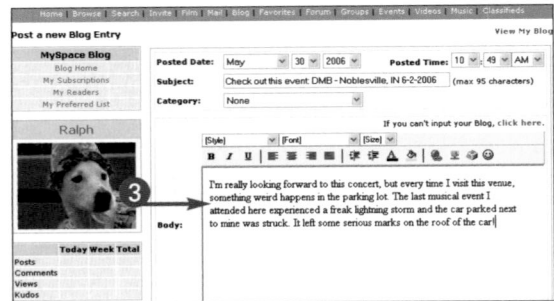

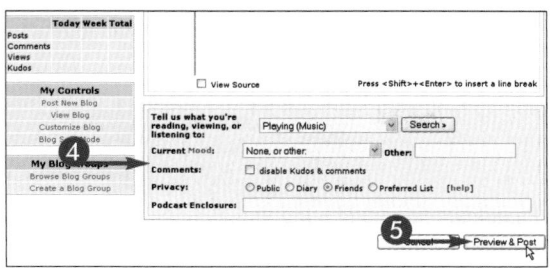

④ Set any blog options you want to assign.

⑤ Click Preview & Post.

The Confirm Blog Posting page appears.

⑥ Review your blog text and click Post Blog.

● To edit the text, click here and make any changes.

● To cancel the entry, click here.

MySpace posts the blog.

TIP

Remove It!

Once you post a blog, you can revisit it to make changes to the text, or you can remove the blog entry entirely. To view your blog, visit the Blog home page and click the View My Blog link. This opens your blog entry. Click the Edit link to make changes to the blog, or click the Remove link to delete the blog.

Send a Bulletin for an Event

You can use MySpace event bulletins to alert your friends and network to upcoming events. For example, you might send out a bulletin to announce an upcoming band gig or a school event.

When you create an event bulletin, MySpace includes the original event information, such as who is hosting the event, and the date and location of the event. You can add additional information to the bulletin.

Once you post the bulletin, all the users in your Friends list receive the information and can view the bulletin.

---

① **Display the event page you want to blog.**

Note: *See the "Add an Event to Your Calendar" task to learn how to view event information.*

② **Click the Bulletin This link.**

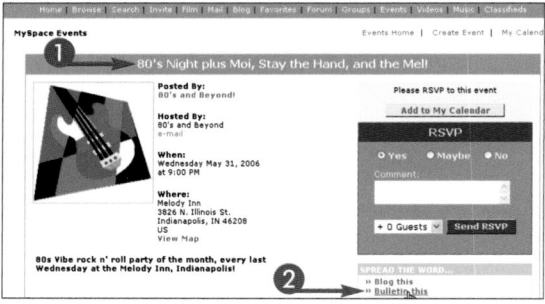

The Post Bulletin form appears.

● By default, the Post Bulletin form includes all the relevant event information.

③ **Type in any additional text you want to send.**

④ **Click Post.**

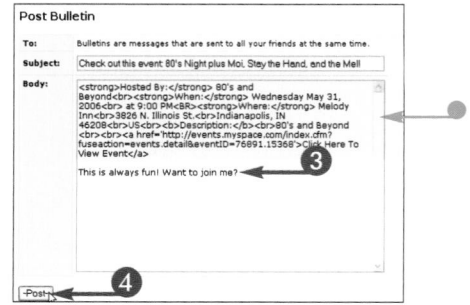

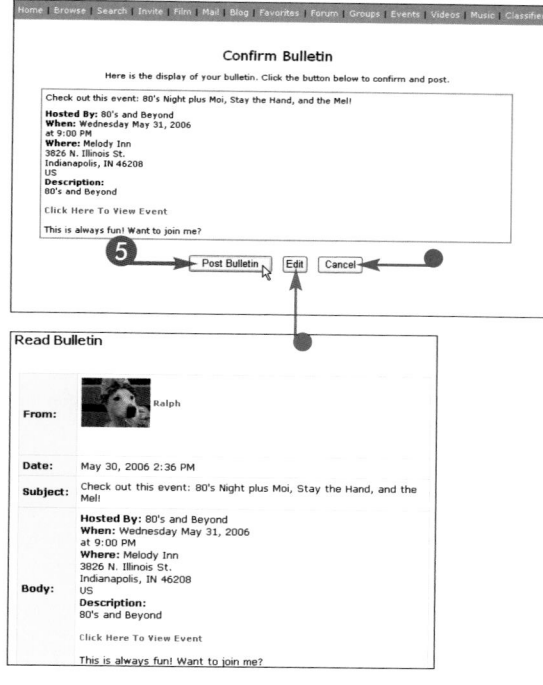

The Confirm Bulletin page appears.

⑤ Review the bulletin and click Post Bulletin.

● To edit the text, click here and make any changes.

● To cancel the entry, click here.

MySpace posts the bulletin.

Other users on your Friends list can now view the bulletin.

Remove It!

You can delete bulletins you receive from other users. Simply open the bulletin, and then click the Delete button to remove it from the list. Once you delete a bulletin, it no longer appears on the My Bulletin Space area of your home page.

Maintaining Privacy on MySpace

You can tap into a variety of privacy features on MySpace to enhance your online safety while using this popular networking site. The best way to protect yourself online is to avoid giving out personal information. In addition, you can change certain MySpace account settings to help keep your privacy. For example, you may want to start protecting yourself from unsolicited invites and IMs.

In this chapter, you learn how to hide your online status, and control who views your calendar, who sends you group invitations, who is allowed to post comments or send instant messages, and more. MySpace continues to add more safety features as needed, so be sure to check the Account Settings page for future updates.

Quick Tips

Hide Your Online Status

You can hide your online status from other MySpace users and surf the site without your friends knowing you are online. Hiding your online status can prevent interruptions, such as instant messages, from other users. You might also hide your online status if you are pestered by spam or unwarranted comments from unknown members during one of your online sessions. When you hide your status, you do not appear online to other users.

You can use the My Account Settings form to control whether your online status is hidden. The My Privacy Settings form offers several options for controlling your privacy.

① In MySpace, click Home.
② Click Account Settings.

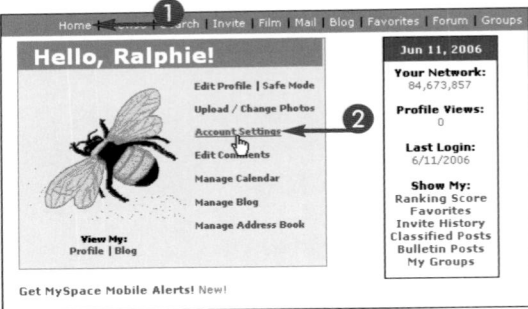

The Change Account Settings page appears.

③ Next to Privacy Settings, click Change Settings.

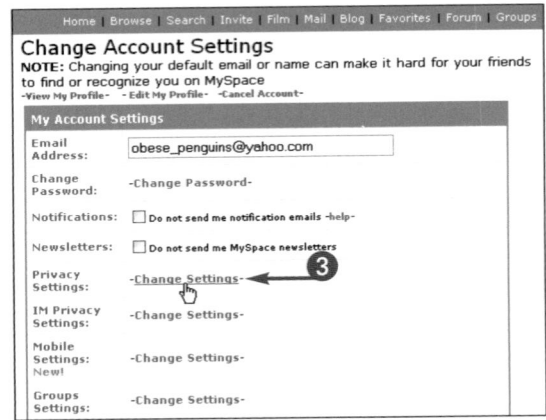

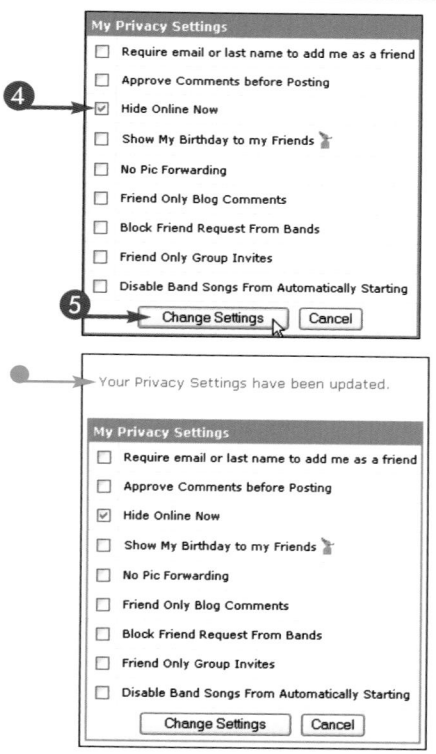

The My Privacy Settings form appears.

4 Click Hide Online Now (☐ changes to ☑).

5 Click Change Settings.

● MySpace updates the settings and you no longer appear to be online.

Important!
If you want to be visible online again, do not forget to unhide your online status. To turn the privacy setting off, simply revisit the My Privacy Settings form and click the Hide Online Now check box (☑ changes to ☐) to turn the feature off. Click the Change Settings button to apply the new setting.

Hide Your Last Login Date

You can hide your last login date so other MySpace users viewing your profile cannot detect when you were last online. You might hide your login date to prevent others from knowing how actively you are using your MySpace account, or inversely, how inactive you are.

You can use HTML coding to hide the login date on your profile page. You can use the MySpace Safe Mode view of your profile to edit your profile page using CSS (Cascading Style Sheets) coding. The Safe Mode view allows you to enter HTML/DHTML and CSS coding to your profile without displaying the formatting.

① In MySpace, click Home.

② Click Safe Mode.

The Safe Mode form page appears for your profile.

③ Next to Headline, click Edit.

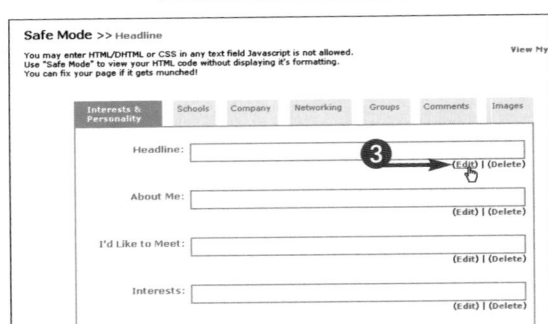

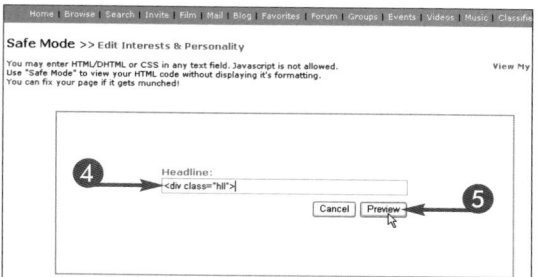

The Headline form field appears.

4 Type `<div class="hll">`.

5 Click Preview.

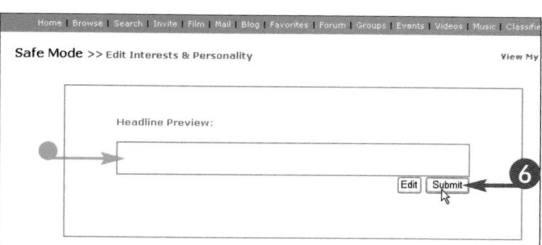

● The Headline Preview field appears blank.

6 Click Submit.

MySpace returns you to the Profile form.

Did You Know?
All Web pages are created with *HTML,* short for HyperText Markup Language. HTML coding instructs a Web browser how to display the data on a page. HTML coding consists of *tags,* which are individual instructions to the browser, surrounded by brackets (<>). If you know HTML, DHTML (Dynamic HyperText Markup Language), or CSS, you can use coding to control the appearance of elements on your MySpace profile page.

continued

Your MySpace profile page uses a table layout structure to display the various elements on the page. Although you cannot change the page layout, you can use CSS coding to change the appearance of the layout. CSS, which stands for Cascading Style Sheets, is a form of HTML coding that allows you to control the appearance of Web page elements.

A CSS style consists of a statement that specifies formatting, such as "make this text blue." It is called cascading because you can use multiple styles all at the same time, and the last style added takes precedence over previous styles.

⑦ Next to About Me, click Edit.

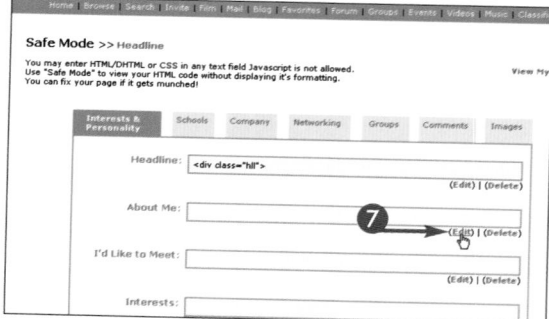

The About Me form appears.

⑧ Type `<style type= "text/css"> div.hll{overflow :hidden; height: 120px;} </style>`.

⑨ Click Preview.

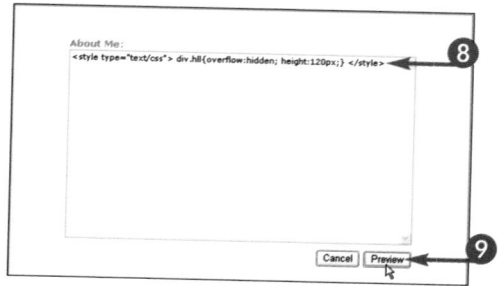

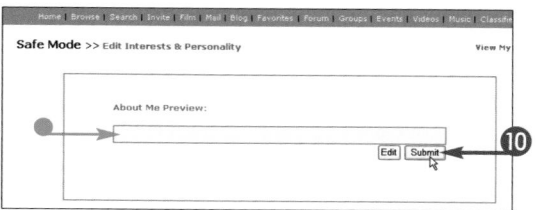

● The About Me Preview field appears blank.

⑩ Click Submit.

MySpace returns you to the Profile form.

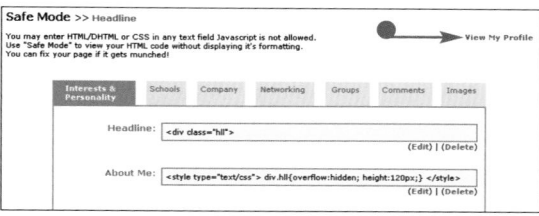

● You can click the View My Profile link to view your profile without the login data.

Delete It!
To display the last login date again on your profile, you can return to Safe Mode and delete the CSS coding from the profile fields in which it is added.

You can use the MySpace Calendar feature to help you keep track of events, appointments, parties, concerts, and more. By default, your MySpace Calendar is set for sharing with friends, which means any entries you make on the calendar are viewable on your profile page by friends who view your page. You can turn off calendar sharing to keep your calendar entries private.

You can control calendar sharing through the Account Settings feature. You can set calendar sharing to Disabled, Share w/Friends, or Share w/Everyone. If you set the option to Share w/Everyone, anyone viewing your profile can see your calendar items.

① In MySpace, click Home.

② Click Account Settings.

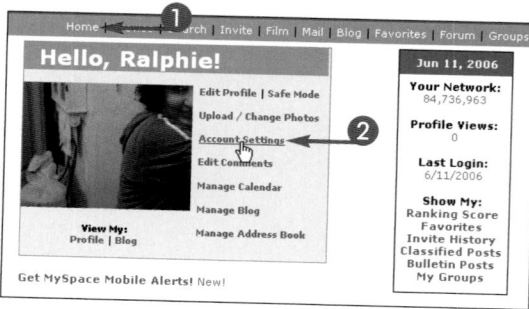

The Change Account Settings page appears.

③ Next to Calendar Settings, click Change Settings.

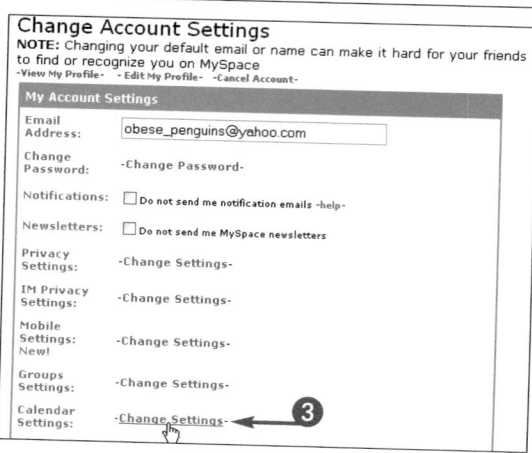

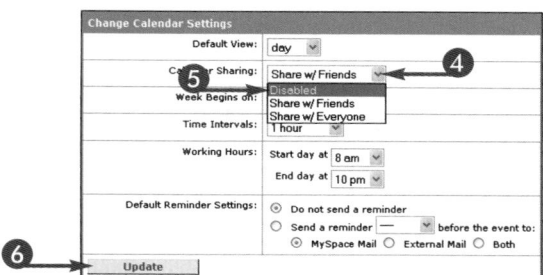

The Change Calendar Settings form appears.

④ Click the Calendar Sharing drop-down arrow.

⑤ Click Disabled.

⑥ Click Update.

Note: If you select Share w/Everyone, anyone on MySpace can see your calendar entries when he or she views your profile.

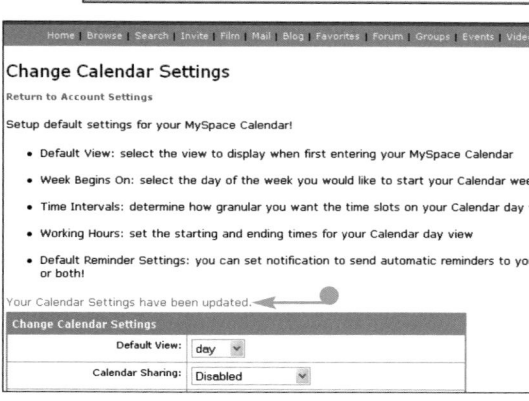

● MySpace updates your settings and displays an update message.

The calendar settings are now only viewable by you.

Note: You can also change the calendar settings by clicking the Options link on the Calendar page.

Did You Know?

You can use the Change Calendar Settings page to set other options for your MySpace Calendar, including setting a default view, and changing time intervals, working hours, and reminder settings.

Allow Group Invitations from Friends Only

MySpace groups are forums dedicated to a particular topic, such as a favorite TV show or hobby. With over two million groups available, you may find yourself receiving unsolicited invitations to join groups that do not interest you. To help keep the invites to a minimum, you can choose to receive only group invites from users on your Friends list. This allows you to check out groups from people you know rather than waste time visiting groups recommended by strangers.

You can use the Change Account Settings form to control privacy settings for invites from others.

① In MySpace, click Home.

② Click Account Settings.

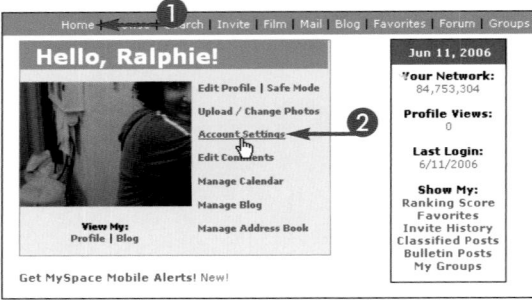

The Change Account Settings page appears.

③ Next to Privacy Settings, click Change Settings.

My Privacy Settings

- ☐ Require email or last name to add me as a friend
- ☐ Approve Comments before Posting
- ☐ Hide Online Now
- ☐ Show My Birthday to my Friends
- ☐ No Pic Forwarding
- ☐ Friend Only Blog Comments
- ☐ Block Friend Request From Bands
- ☑ Friend Only Group Invites
- ☐ Disable Band Songs From Automatically Starting

[Change Settings] [Cancel]

The My Privacy Settings form appears.

④ Click Friend Only Group Invites (☐ changes to ☑).

⑤ Click Change Settings.

Your Privacy Settings have been updated.

My Privacy Settings

- ☐ Require email or last name to add me as a friend
- ☐ Approve Comments before Posting
- ☐ Hide Online Now
- ☐ Show My Birthday to my Friends
- ☐ No Pic Forwarding
- ☐ Friend Only Blog Comments
- ☐ Block Friend Request From Bands
- ☑ Friend Only Group Invites
- ☐ Disable Band Songs From Automatically Starting

[Change Settings] [Cancel]

● MySpace updates the settings and displays an update message.

You can no longer receive unsolicited group invites.

TIP

Did You Know?
You can change how MySpace denotes new group posts or bulletins on the Groups home page. By default, MySpace is set up to indicate new group posts with an icon in the New Group Posts box on the Groups home page. To turn off indicators, display the Change Account Settings page, and then click the Change Settings link next to Group Settings. Next, click the check box to turn the feature off (☑ changes to ☐) and click Change Settings to apply the change.

When you allow others to view your MySpace profile page, they can leave comments on your page. If you find yourself receiving too many unwanted comments, you can control your privacy setting for comments. You can turn on an option that allows you to approve or deny comments before they are posted to your profile.

When you activate the Approve Comments Before Posting option, MySpace sends any comments to you in the form of an e-mail message. You can then read the comment and decide whether to approve or deny the addition to your profile's comments section.

① In MySpace, click Home.
② Click Account Settings.

The Change Account Settings page appears.

③ Next to Privacy Settings, click Change Settings.

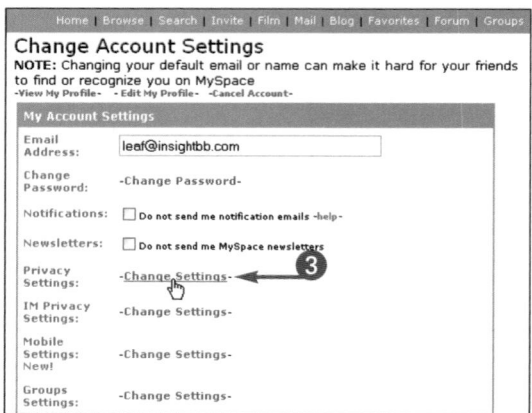

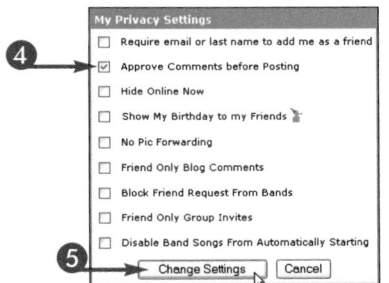

The My Privacy Settings form appears.

④ **Click Approve Comments Before Posting**
(☐ changes to ☑).

⑤ **Click Change Settings.**

Date:	Jun 11, 2006 9:04 PM	Flag spam/abuse. [?
Subject:	Request to Approve Comment	
Body:	Ralphie has posted a new comment about you on MySpace!	

MySpace updates the settings.

● The next time someone tries to add a comment to your profile, you receive an e-mail that allows you to approve or deny the comment.

According to your privacy settings, all comments must be approved by you before they appear on your profile.

Ralphie's Comment:

"I, too, admire your attire!"

Please click the link below to approve or deny this comment.

⦿ **Approve, or**

◯ **Deny**

[Submit]

Ralphie

TIP

Did You Know?
You can remove comments posted to your profile, or add your own comments to the mix. To remove a comment, click the Edit Comments link on your home page to open the View Comments page. Click the Delete link next to the comment you want to remove. To add your own comment, click the Add Comment link.

Allow Instant Messages from Friends Only

Instant messages, or IMs for short, are an important part of the MySpace community, but not all IMs are welcome. If you find yourself receiving too many unwelcome IMs, you can turn off the messages entirely, or choose to receive IMs only from people in your Friends list.

When you first create your MySpace account, IMs are turned off by default. In order to enable them, you must change the options on the My IM Privacy Settings form. The form offers three options: no IMs, IMs only from friends, or IMs from anyone.

① In MySpace, click Home.

② Click Account Settings.

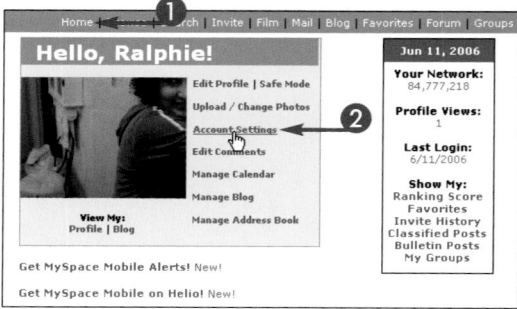

The Change Account Settings page appears.

③ Next to IM Privacy Settings, click Change Settings.

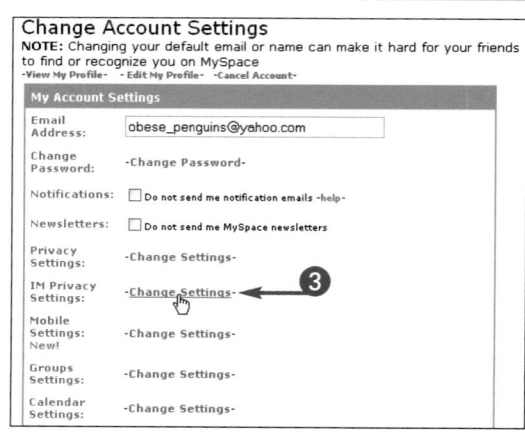

The My IM Privacy Settings form appears.

④ Click Only Friends Can IM Me (☐ changes to ☑).

⑤ Click Change Settings.

MySpace updates your settings.

If a user tries to IM you, a prompt appears stating that you do not receive IMs.

Did You Know?

If you are having trouble with a particular MySpace user, you can add the person to your Blocked User list. To do so, visit the person's profile page, and then click the Block User link. This adds the user's name to your Blocked User list. To view the list at any time from the home page, click Account Settings, and then click Blocked Users.

Blogging is one of the most popular activities to do on MySpace. However, once you post a blog, it is available for anyone to see. You can control who views your blog by creating a preferred list of users who are permitted to read your work. As long as you know the name of the person you want to allow to view the blog, you can add the person to your preferred list.

You can manage your blog and your preferred blog list through the Blog page. The Blog Control Center page displays links for creating new blogs, customizing blogs, and managing a preferred list of readers.

① In MySpace, click Blog.

② Click My Preferred List.

The My Private List page appears.

③ Click Find User To Be Added to Your Private List.

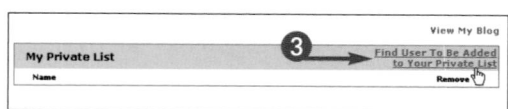

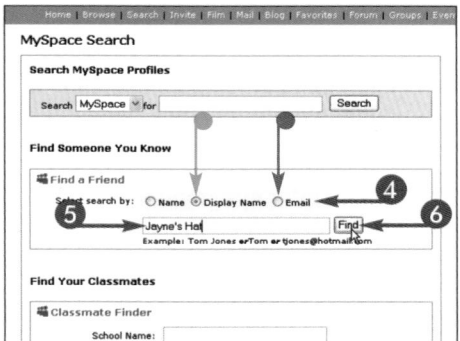

The MySpace Search page appears.

④ Click the type of search you want to conduct (○ changes to ◉).

● To search for a known username, click Display Name.

● If you know your friend's e-mail, you can conduct a search using his or her e-mail address.

⑤ Type your friend's display name here.

⑥ Click Find.

MySpace displays the search results.

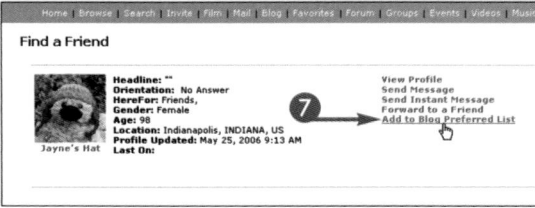

⑦ Click Add to Blog Preferred List.

MySpace adds the user to your My Private List on the Blog page.

Delete It!

To remove a user from the My Private List for blog readers, return to the Blog home page and click the My Preferred List link. This opens the My Private List page listing all of the preferred readers of your blog. To remove a user, simply click the Remove link next to the user's name.

If you prefer to keep your blog posts private, you can use the MySpace blogging feature much like your own personal diary. For example, you may find your current blog too personal to share. Rather than posting it for the general public, you can turn the entry into your own private post, which only you can read.

You can choose from four different privacy settings when creating a blog: Public, Diary, Friends, or Preferred List. Ordinarily, when you create a blog post, anyone who views your profile can view the blog. The Public option is set by default unless you specify another privacy setting.

① In MySpace, click Blog.

② Click Post New Blog.

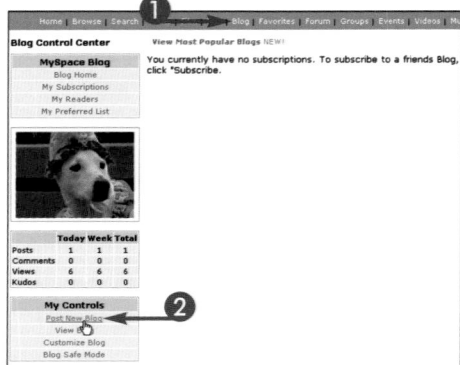

The Post a New Blog Entry page appears.

③ Fill out your blog entry.

④ Under Privacy settings, click Diary (○ changes to ◉).

⑤ Click Preview & Post.

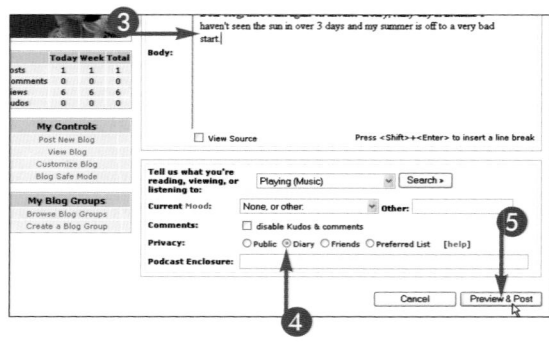

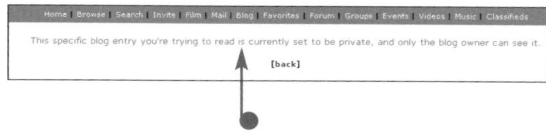

The Confirm Blog Posting page appears.

⑥ Click Post Blog.

● To edit the blog, click Edit and make any changes.

● If a user tries to view your private blog, MySpace displays this message.

Note: *The subject of all your blog entries appears on your profile regardless of whether the blog is public or private.*

Delete It!
You can remove a private blog, or change the privacy setting for the post. To do so, view the blog entry and click the Remove link. To edit the entry instead, click the Edit link to open the Edit a Blog Entry page and change the privacy setting.

Turn Off MySpace Notifications

You can control how MySpace sends notifications to your regular e-mail address. Among your account setting options are controls for specifying how MySpace notifications are sent. Ordinarily, when you receive a message from another MySpace user, a comment on your profile or blog, or a friend request, MySpace sends you a notification. If you prefer not to receive these notifications, you can turn them off.

Even with notifications turned off, you can still receive messages through the MySpace mail system.

① In MySpace, click Home.

② Click Account Settings.

The Change Account Settings page appears.

③ Next to Notifications, click Do Not Send Me Notification E-mails (☐ changes to ☑).

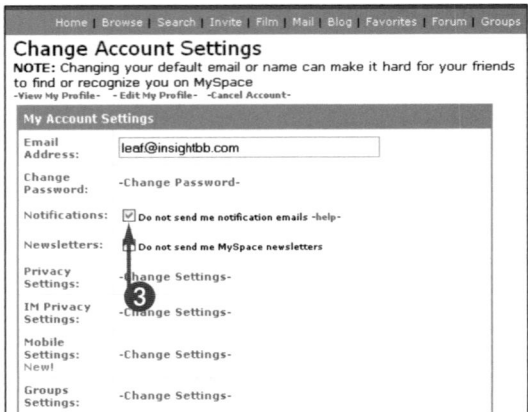

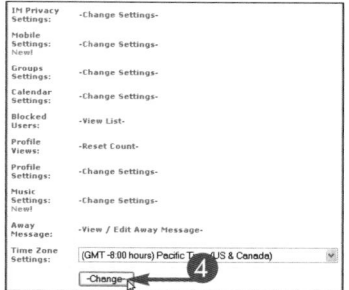

④ Scroll to the bottom of the form and click Change.

MySpace updates your settings.

● You can still view messages through the MySpace Mail Center Inbox.

Did You Know?

By default, your MySpace account settings are also set up to receive the MySpace newsletter. If you prefer not to receive the newsletter, you can turn the setting off. Open the Change Account Settings page and click the Do Not Send Me MySpace Newsletters check box (☐ changes to ☑) next to the Newsletters setting. Click Change to apply the new setting.

Enhancing MySpace Security

MySpace is hugely popular, with tens of millions of users. For the most part, MySpace is generally a fun and friendly site with a lot of interesting content for people of all ages. However, as with any large collection of people, MySpace has its share of malicious and nefarious users. These people put up profiles that display salacious content, write comments containing profanity, or send spam messages.

To protect yourself and your family, you need to understand these threats and know what you can do to thwart them. For example, you can block friend requests that come from people who do not know you, and you can disable or vet blog comments. Fortunately, MySpace offers these and quite a few other options that you can use to minimize security threats.

Quick Tips

To protect your children on MySpace means to understand the dangers that await your children and to learn ways to avoid those dangers.

Teenagers are flocking to MySpace because it is a great way for young people to express themselves, stay in touch with friends, and make new friends.

Unfortunately, it is very easy for children to come upon inappropriate material on MySpace, even inadvertently. This is why the MySpace terms of service insist that members be at least 14 years old. However, even for teenagers, you should not underestimate the level of protection that they need.

Supervise Your Kids

Ideally, parents should be directly involved in protecting their children on MySpace. No teenager will allow a parent to directly supervise his or her MySpace sessions, of course, but that does not mean parents cannot be involved. Setting limits on when and how long young teens use MySpace is a good start. You should also talk to your kids about what they have seen and done on MySpace, and you should view their profiles to see how they are presenting themselves.

Educate Your Kids

The most important thing you can do to keep your children safe on MySpace is to educate them on the potential dangers. Children are naïve and make friends easily, so you need to caution them that other MySpace members may misrepresent themselves by lying about their age, gender, or location. Parents should lay down ground rules for using MySpace, including the rules listed on the following page. Kids should also know how to block users and perform other security tasks, as described in this chapter.

Avoid Personal Information

A MySpace profile is a chance to express yourself, and most teens enjoy doing that, particularly in the relatively anonymous setting that MySpace provides. However, you should caution your children not to include in their profile or blog any information that would enable a stranger to locate their home or school.

Avoid Embarrassing Information

Many kids think that only their friends can see their profile. You should warn your kids that anyone can view a MySpace profile, even people who are not MySpace members. This means that kids should not post profile data, blog entries, photos, or comments that might be embarrassing.

Do Not Agree to Meet Strangers

Make sure your kids know that just because someone is on their Friends list, that person is not necessarily a real friend, so they should not attempt to meet people they do not know personally. Make sure your kids know that they must tell you immediately if a stranger asks to meet them.

Report Inappropriate Content

Make sure your kids know that they should never respond to spam or to someone who sends them an abusive or inappropriate message. Instead, they should immediately report the inappropriate behavior to the MySpace authorities, as described later in this chapter.

Protecting yourself on MySpace means taking a few sensible precautions to avoid the negative aspects of MySpace.

After you create a MySpace account, within a few hours you will receive a few friend requests and a few requests to join groups. You will also receive your first spam messages, because MySpace, like the Web as a whole, has its share of spammers, scammers, and malicious members. To ensure that this dark side of MySpace does not ruin your MySpace experience, you should keep security in mind at all times, and observe a few common-sense precautions to keep yourself out of trouble.

Watch Your Content

You are free to post anything you want to your profile, as long as you honor the MySpace terms of service. However, if you put up provocative pictures of yourself, or post inflammatory material, then chances are good that you will get a lot of comments, perhaps to the point of harassment.

Check Profiles

If you receive a friend request, always click the profile graphic in the From column that appears in the Friend Request Manager window. This will take you to the requester's profile, so you can see if the member is a spammer or someone equally inappropriate.

Check Groups

If you receive a request to join a group, be sure to check out the group thoroughly before clicking the Join Group button. Read the group introduction and read some recent posts to see if the group is appropriate for you.

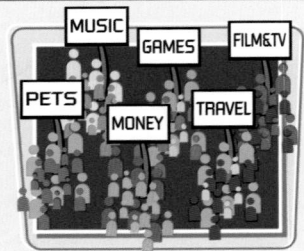

Do Not Post Confidential Data

There are people who troll MySpace looking for confidential data that they can use for their own advantage. Spammers, for example, look for e-mail addresses in blogs and comments. Therefore, never include a legitimate e-mail address in a post, and never post data such as company secrets, credit card data, and so on.

Do Not Assume Anonymity

It may seem that MySpace members and the general public know you only by your profile's display name, but that does not necessarily mean you are anonymous. There may be clues in your blog posts, comments, or other entries that could identify you to a determined snoop. Therefore, do not post anything (such as a diatribe against your boss) that could come back to haunt you.

Do Not Respond to Spam

If you receive a friend request from a spammer, ignore the request. Also, never send a message to a member who spams you, or you will just get more spam. Never click a Web site link that appears within a spam. The link may take you to a site that displays objectionable content or that surreptitiously installs spyware on your computer.

Know Your Options

The best way to enhance your MySpace security and privacy is to know what options MySpace offers. The most important privacy settings are covered in Chapter 8, and the most important security settings are covered in the rest of this chapter.

You can greatly reduce the number of inappropriate or nuisance friend requests you get by allowing only requests to come from people who know you.

MySpace is all about meeting new friends. One of the most common ways to do that is to check out someone's profile and, if you like what you see, click the Add to Friends link in the Contact table.

However, any MySpace member can do that, so you may receive a lot of requests from people you have no interest in or from spammers or scammers.

If you are tired of such requests, you can configure your account to accept requests only from people who know your last name or your e-mail address.

① In MySpace, click Home.

② Click Account Settings.

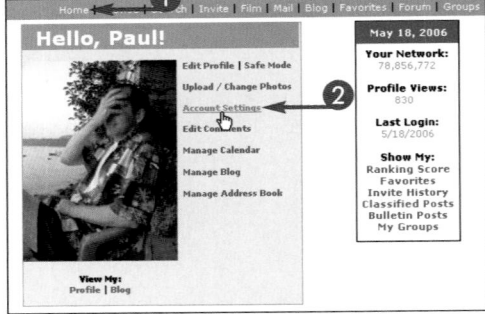

The Change Account Settings window appears.

③ Next to Privacy Settings, click Change Settings.

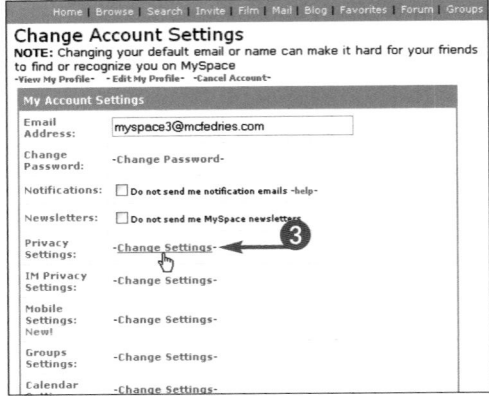

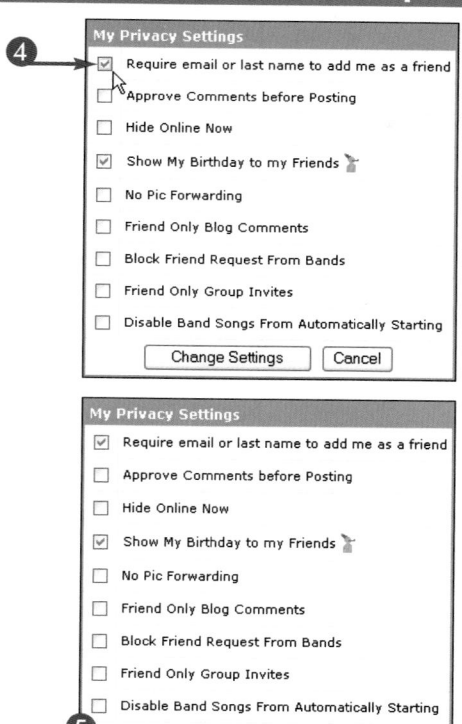

The My Privacy Settings window appears.

④ **Click Require Email or Last Name to Add Me as a Friend** (☐ changes to ☑).

⑤ Click Change Settings.

MySpace now blocks friend requests from people who do not know you.

More Options!

You can also set up your account so that only your friends can view the full profile. Follow Steps **1** to **3** to display the Privacy Settings window. In the Who Can View My Full Profile section, click My Friends Only (☐ changes to ☑). Click Change Settings to put the new setting into effect. People who are not your fiends will see only your name, picture, and basic information.

You can reduce the number of friend requests you have to deal with by blocking requests that come from bands.

One of the pleasures of MySpace is the wide variety of music available via the thousands of band profiles. Not surprisingly, bands like to have a lot of friends, because that enables them to send bulletins and messages about new releases

and live shows to a lot of people. Therefore, most MySpace members receive a steady stream of friend requests from bands.

If you never accept such requests, or prefer to find bands on your own, you can configure your account to block all friend requests that come from band profiles.

① In MySpace, click Home.

② Click Account Settings.

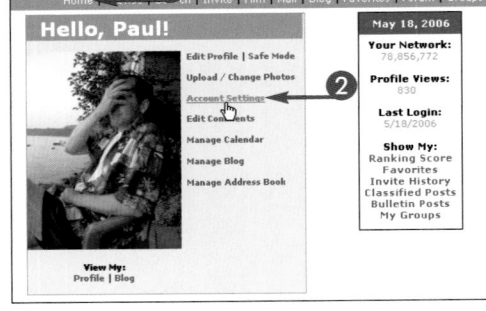

The Change Account Settings window appears.

③ Next to Privacy Settings, click Change Settings.

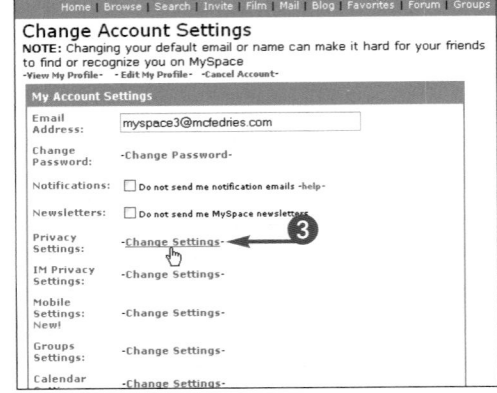

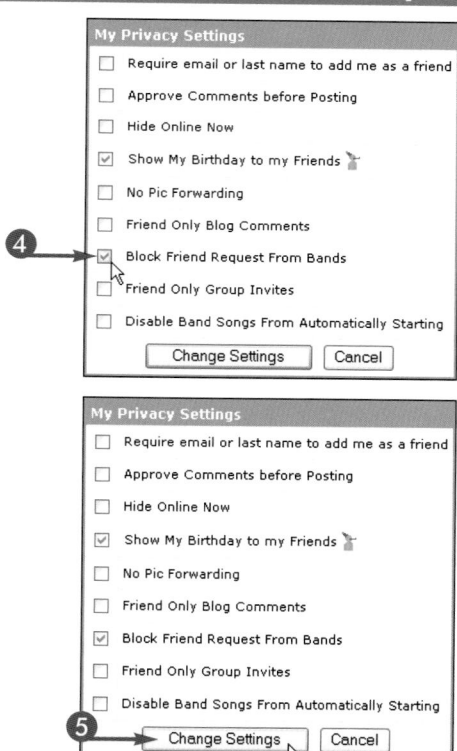

The My Privacy Settings window appears.

④ Click Block Friend Requests From Bands (☐ changes to ☑).

⑤ Click Change Settings.

MySpace now blocks friend requests from bands.

More Options!
If you want to be friends with a band, your best bet is to locate the band's profile and send a friend request. Few bands will turn you down. Click Music in the navigation bar, locate the band, and then click Add to Friends in the Contact table.

Disable Comments for a Blog Post

You can avoid potentially dangerous blog post comments by disabling comments when you create the post.

Each MySpace blog post comes with an Add Comment link that enables readers to post their own reactions or opinions concerning the entry. This is a big part of the MySpace "conversation," and most comments are innocuous. However, it is possible for readers to include links in comments, and those links may take users to Web sites that attempt to install malware, phish for confidential data, or display offensive content.

If you are concerned about such security risks, remember that you can delete any comment by clicking its Remove link. If this happens frequently, you can configure a blog post to display comments. Note that it disables kudos, as well.

1. In MySpace, click Home.
2. Click Blog.

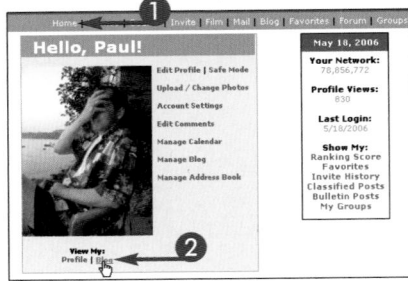

Your MySpace blog appears.

3. Click Post New Blog.

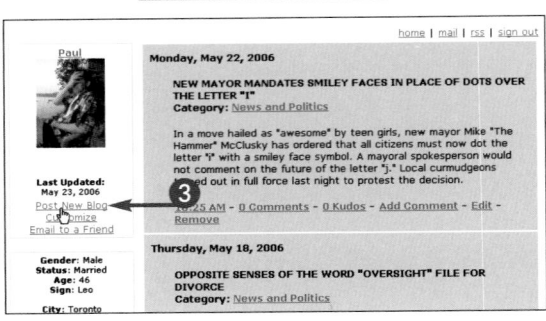

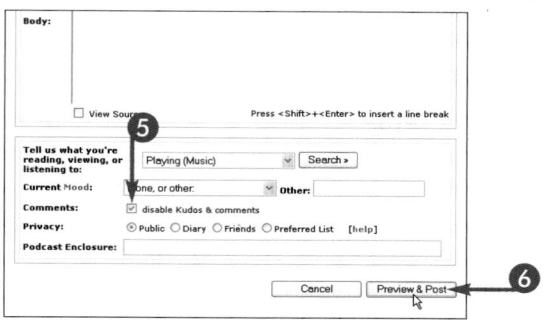

The Post a New Blog Entry window appears.

④ Create the blog post.

⑤ Click Disable Kudos & Comments (☐ changes to ☑).

⑥ Click Preview & Post.

The Confirm Blog Posting window appears.

⑦ Click Post Blog.

MySpace posts the entry with comments and kudos disabled.

More Options!
You can also disable comments for an existing blog post. Follow Steps **1** and **2** to display your posts. Find the post with which you want to work and then click its Edit link. Click the Disable Kudos & Comments check box (☐ changes to ☑), click Preview & Post, and then click Post Blog.

You can avoid comments that contain objectionable material or spam by approving all comments before posting them.

MySpace users can add comments to your profile, pictures, or blog posts. Profile and picture comments are usually benign because only your friends can post such comments. However, anyone can comment on your blog posts. This means that you may occasionally get comments

that contain inappropriate content, spam, or even links to malicious Web sites. You can avoid such comments by configuring your account to approve all comments before posting them. When a reader posts a comment, he or she sees the following message:

"This user requires all comments to be approved before being posted. Your comment has been submitted to this user for approval."

1 In MySpace, click Home.

2 Click Account Settings.

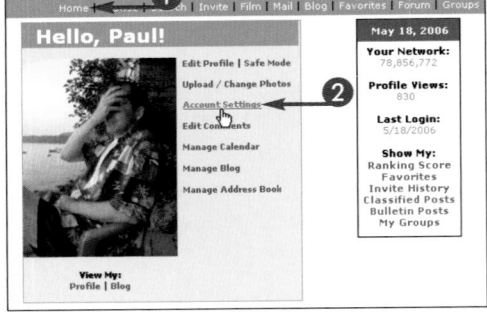

The Change Account Settings window appears.

3 Next to Privacy Settings, click Change Settings.

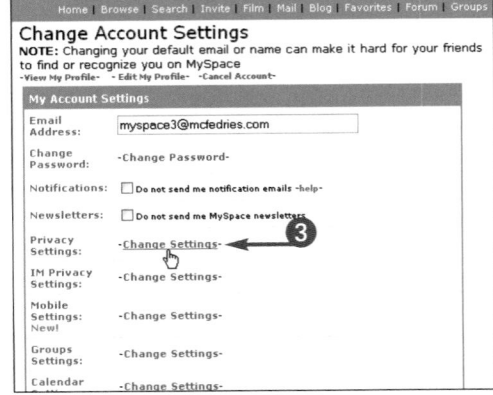

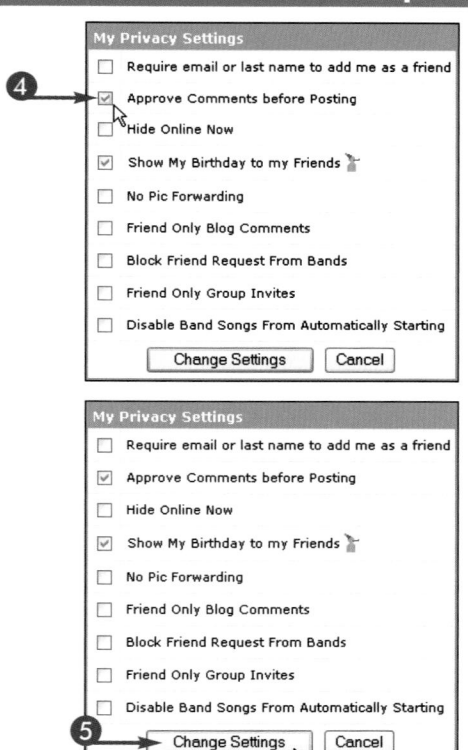

The My Privacy Settings window appears.

④ Click Approve Comments Before Posting
(☐ changes to ☑).

⑤ Click Change Settings.

MySpace now enables you to approve comments before posting them.

Try It!

When a reader submits a comment, you receive a MySpace Mail message with the subject line "Request to Approve Blog Comment." Open the message and read the comment. If you do not want to post the comment, click Deny (○ changes to ⊙) and then click Submit.

You can make comments on your MySpace site more secure by disabling HTML.

When users comment on your profile, pictures, or blog posts, they can use HTML to insert images, Flash movies, and links. This HTML is not usually a problem in profile or picture comments because only friends can post comments on those items. However, any reader can comment on your blog posts. You can use the steps in the previous task to approve all comments, but you may find that time consuming. In that case, you can still make comments more secure by disabling HTML. This prevents users from inserting images, movies, and links in their comments.

① In MySpace, click Home.

② Click Account Settings.

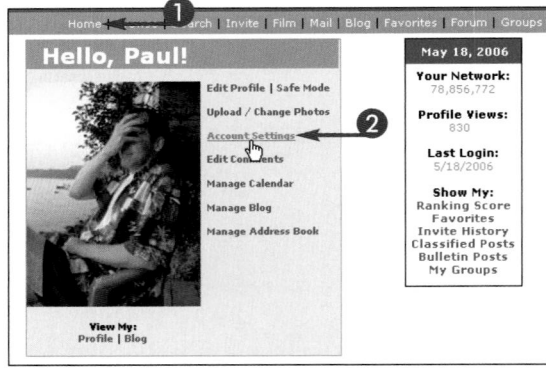

The Change Account Settings window appears.

③ Next to Profile Settings, click Change Settings.

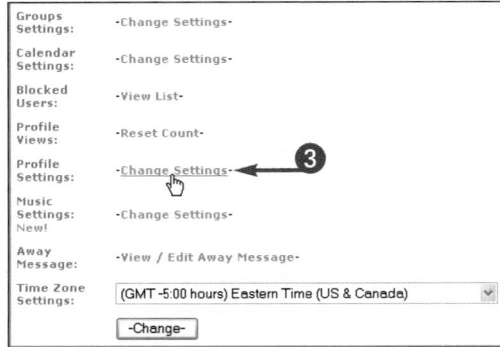

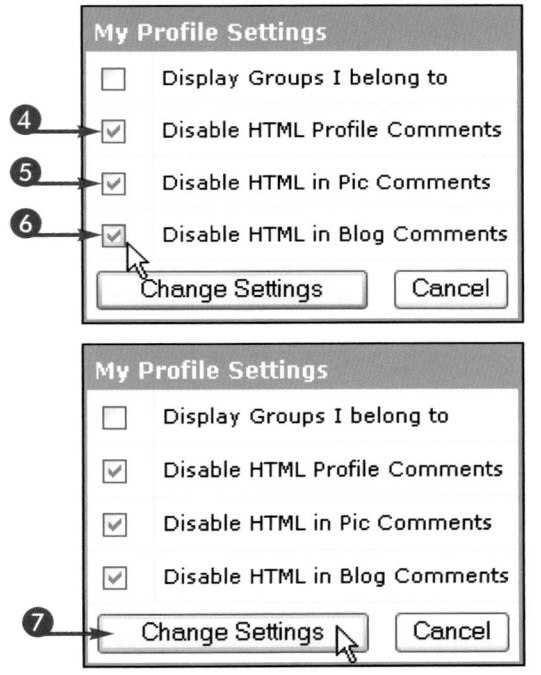

The My Profile Settings window appears.

4️⃣ Click Disable HTML Profile Comments (☐ changes to ☑).

5️⃣ Click Disable HTML in Pic Comments (☐ changes to ☑).

6️⃣ Click Disable HTML in Blog Comments (☐ changes to ☑).

7️⃣ Click Change Settings.

MySpace disables HTML in all comments.

(TIP)

Try It!
In addition to disabling HTML for picture comments, you may also want to prevent users from e-mailing your pictures to other people. Follow Steps **1** and **2**, click Change Settings (next to Privacy Settings), click No Pic Forwarding (☐ changes to ☑), and then click Change Settings.

You can prevent a MySpace member from contacting you by blocking that person.

Most MySpace members are good people who honestly want to broaden their online horizons by connecting with others who share similar interests, musical tastes, and so on. However, with tens of millions of members, you are bound to come across your fair share of hucksters,

spammers, creeps, and people who are simply annoying.

Fortunately, MySpace gives you a powerful weapon to deal with any of these people who repeatedly pester you with friend requests, messages, or bulletins: You can block the user, and MySpace will ensure that any communication from that person does not reach your MySpace mailbox.

---

① Click Mail.

② Click Friend Requests.

The Friend Request Manager window appears.

● If you have a message from the user, click Inbox instead.

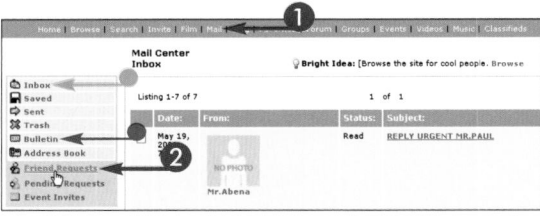

● If you have a bulletin from the user, click Bulletin instead.

③ In the From field, click the user you want to block.

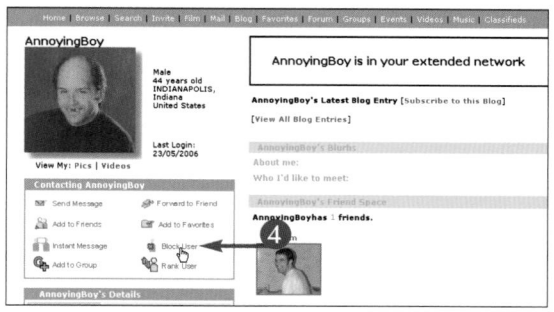

The user's profile appears.

④ In the Contact table, click Block User.

MySpace asks you to confirm that you want to block the user.

⑤ Click OK.

MySpace adds the user to your Blocked list.

Reverse It!

If you block a user by accident, or decide to give a blocked user a second chance, you can unblock the user. Click Home, click Account Settings, and then click View List (next to Blocked Users). In the list of blocked users, click the Unblock User link next to the user you want to unblock.

You can help MySpace rid its system of spam and offensive messages by flagging such messages.

Most of the MySpace messages you get will be from friends, members interested in being your friend, people curious about your profile, and system messages from "Tom."

However, just as the e-mail system as a whole is rife with spam and other useless messages, so too is the MySpace mail

system. It is an unfortunate fact of MySpace life that you will receive your share of spam, as well as offensive or abusive messages from some of the less-evolved members.

To help combat such messages, MySpace enables you to flag such messages as spam or as having abusive content. MySpace analyzes flagged messages in an effort to reduce the amount of improper mail sent through the system.

① Click Mail.

② Click Inbox.

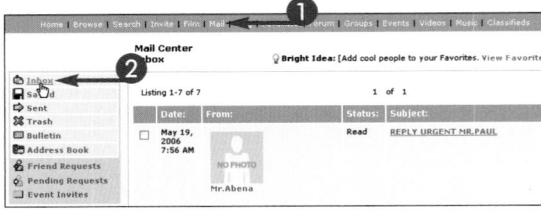

Your MySpace Inbox appears.

③ In the Subject field, click the subject line of the message you want to flag.

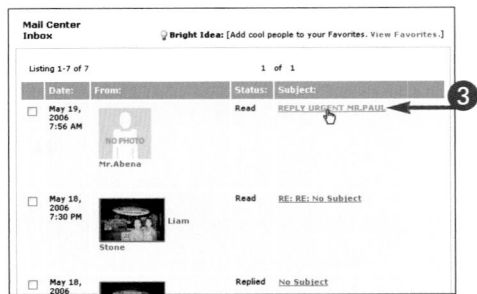

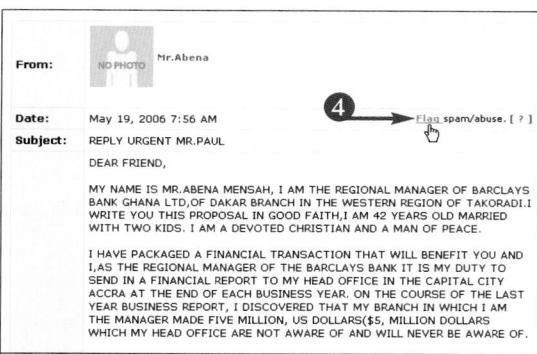

The Read Mail window appears.

④ Click Flag.

MySpace asks you to confirm that you want to flag the message.

⑤ Click OK.

Caution!

If a message that is clearly spam offers a link to a Web site, do not click the link. Such sites often attempt to install spyware or other malicious programs. Also, immediately flag any messages that ask you for your MySpace password or confidential data such as your credit card number or bank PIN number.

Index

continued

Index

Index